TEACHABLE MOMENTS WITH Dr. ABC:

A SPOONFUL FOR THE JOURNEY

Dr. Andrew B. Campbell

ACKNOWLEDGEMENTS

I wish to thank my Facebook followers whose engagement and interaction with my *"Teachable Moments with Dr. ABC"* page is invaluable, motivating, and provided much fuel for the journey.

I wish to also say a very special thanks to a number of people who offered their help and insights in very significant and tangible ways during this process - Keishla Hunt-Wilson, Kaschka Watson, Stacey Richards, Tehmina Khan, Andreia Florea, Franca Esposito, Reena Soin, Delon Francis and my wonderful cousin Joan Campbell. I am forever grateful for all the help and assistance you all gave me. You have proven to me that there are indeed unselfish people in this world who want as much for others as they want for themselves.

To my inner circle of friends, your prayers, encouragement and support have been the undercurrent throughout this process. You all come into my life at different parts of the journey and I am constantly reminded that I am surrounded by good people and I have reaped far more than I have sowed in these relationships and friendships.

Finally, I wish to give thanks to The Man Upstairs, for taking me so far and allowing this little boy from Waterford to continue realizing his dreams!

DEDICATION

To powerful women who helped to frame my journey in very special ways, who came into my life at very pivotal times and gave me the spoonful I needed for my journey:

My grandmother, **Sister May (RIP)** – I admire the power, strength, and influence she demonstrated in everything she did. I desire to be that impactful.
***
My mother, **Doris Adina Campbell** – You are the best example of a mother and a Christian that I know.
***
My dance teacher, **Jennifer Garwood** – You opened your arms, heart, and dance troupe just when I needed somewhere to belong.
***
My first boss, **Barbara Reid** – You saw so much in me at age 16, believed in me, and trusted me with so much. I am sure that nothing I have accomplished in life today is a shock to you – you were my cheerleader when I was not even in the game.
***
My friend, **Keishla Hunt-Wilson** – I believe God brings the right people into your life, at the right time, for the right reasons, and you are my proof of that. Thanks!
***
My friend, **Lorraine Simms (Simmsy)** - A friend who came into my life and has been nothing less than a cheerleader. One of the kindest people I know.

Introduction: Journey With Me

This book is a collection of my writings from my Facebook page. It is a collection of my honest reflections as I journey from day to day. I chose to name this volume, "A *Spoonful for the Journey*," as I believe that in life we all need a little bit more of something to take us to where we are going. That spoonful for some may be inspiration, motivation, or confrontation. For others, it is reflection, revival or restoration. For others, it is a rebuke, reproof or a strong reminder. Whatever it is that you need, I believe that these reflections will offer each of you something special on your journey. So come journey with me!

"One of the best teachers we had, one who spoke life and impacted everyone within our classroom. So many of our classmates are looking forward to pursuing their Masters after that talk in our classroom. Keep walking in purpose because you will never know the hope you are giving to someone who is getting ready to throw in the towel." **Kara**

> *"DR . ABC. ...Continue to grow, glow and go."* **Romer**

"Authentic and powerful." **Khary**

> *"Boy, so simple yet deep. Makes you go hummmmmm. I am so happy you had loving arms to fall into. Your message is solid. Invest in friends."* **Ann-Marie**

"One of your finest notes Andy!" **Chenayi**

> *"You made me cry today, Andrew. I never did on Mother's Day when I reflected on my mother's ordeal to care for us as a single mother. It is very heartbreaking knowing she never lived to benefit from her seeds. May her soul rest in peace. Mothers Rock!!!!"* **Jacinth**

" I am encouraged, thank you my brother, this is my spiritual vitamin for today." **Audrey**

"On time...on time...on time...Have a wonderful day today."
Jan Viana

"To find the kind of friends who are willing to ask "show me where it hurts" and listen to you, is almost impossible in today's society. I find a lot of times we just find it easier to wear a mask; a mask that hides all the sadness, worries, and the hurt we carry inside."
Karina

"This is deep! Wow, moved by this, hurting inside is real, going through this at present." **Sagapoe**

"Amen, Andrew. I watched that girl shine at both concerts and thought how wonderful it was for her to be part of her peer group, integrated in a program where everyone shares the same passion not disability. Her eyes sparkled and her heart beamed! All because of you. Merry Christmas, Andrew!" **Marianne**

Word Power # 1: Resilience

We live in a mean world. The truth is no matter how much we preach and beseech we have people around us that will always serve negativity. We have those around us who will hurt or harm us. We have those around us who can't bear the sight of us, and of course, often times, with no reason. We live in a world where many are bullied, dragged, pushed, and excluded in so many ways. The truth is, I do not believe this will get better. What can we do then if we can't fight all the battles and win all the wars? What can we do then if we cannot make everything right and correct every wrong? What can we do then if we just don't have the time and resource to address every ill or mishap? Here is what I suggest - resilience.

Many of us are way too weak and fickle these days. Everything someone says about us pushes us into depression and distress. We have to learn how to stand. Not just stand, but stand Strong. I was talking to my Principal the other day and he shared with me the words his grandmother taught him, when he was young and complained about issues he was having in general. She told him that we cannot afford to carpet the world so he should buy himself a good pair of slippers.

Yes, resilience is what we need. We must teach ourselves and our children how to become more resilient. We can't cry for everything and we can't call 911 for every ant that crawls across our plate. We have to learn coping, stamina, and standing skills - we must learn resilience.

Dr. ABC

Word Power # 2: Gratitude

Gratitude is like a tonic! Many people don't realize what impact showing gratitude can have on others. There are people who ask you for a favour and, like the nine blind beggars, they never return to say thanks. They don't know the power of gratitude. One thing I notice is that many of us no longer say thanks to our parents, siblings and close friends anymore. We consider their gifts and kindness obligatory and so we forget that they also need to know that we appreciate their efforts. We forget that gratitude gets us more!

I receive many letters, notes, postcards, and emails each year from students who wish to tell me thanks for being a good teacher, online facilitator, or lecturer. I am not sure about other teachers, but what that does for me is push me to be even better. It does not allow me to sit and relax and think I have made it. Instead, it tells me that hundreds more out there want that kind of teaching, desire that level of engagement and need that passionate motivation. It pushes me to sharpen my skills, update my tools, and ignite my fire each time I walk into a new class or sign into a new course online. Gratitude gets them more of me.

I have also been on the other side of gratitude, where others do so much for me – I ensure that they know how valuable their contribution is. Over the years of studying, I have had a few select people who have contributed to my studies in tangible, measurable and significant ways. I tell them thanks many times and show them my gratitude in concrete ways. I know for a fact that they have been motivated to help me even more, since they know how much I value and appreciate their help. Gratitude gets me more.

Gratitude is a tonic! Show gratitude today.

Dr. ABC

Word Power # 3: Plans

I bet if I ask every one of you today about your plans for next week, next month, next summer, next year and the next 5 years, most of you will have a response. You will be excited to share your latest inspirations, your dreams, your ideas and your hopes. Thanks for sharing - but are these actual plans?
We have many ideas and dreams, but why is it that we are failing to plan for them. If you ask many people about their plans for next year, they will give you a whole list of ideas. Well, an idea is not a plan! What are your plans? Have you written down your plans? Have you thought about the resources you will need for this plan? Have you thought about how this plan will impact your present, on-going plans? Have you figured out how this plan will impact those around you?

I know people who "plan" to go back to school, yet they never look at a school website or drop by the admissions office of a college or school - but they are on the computer all day. Others are "planning" for a trip, to buy a car, a home or some major acquisition - but no actual planning has gone into place. Others are "planning" to get married and live happily ever after - yet they are never interested in a date or commitment.

A dream is not a plan
A desire is not a plan
A deep feeling (no matter how deep) is not a plan
A wish is not a plan
A hope is not a plan
An aspiration is not a plan

A plan must have a timeline; it must be specific and measurable. A person looks and examines the pros and cons. Today let us really begin to plan and take all those dreams, ideas, deep feelings, ambitions, wishes, hopes, and aspirations and turn them into real plans.

Dr. ABC

Word Power # 4: Choose What to Carry

I have been travelling for the past 15 years and every time I travel, no matter where I go, I over pack. Many times, when I reach my destination, I am upset as half of the things I do not wear, never needed, or could honestly have done without. This year, for the first time, I really decided to choose what to carry. I put everything I would love to carry on the bed and then I eliminated what I really didn't need to carry. I am learning more and more each day that not everything is needed and not everything is worth carrying.

In this life, there are so many things that confront us, bombard us, attack us, and weigh us down. These things include the weight of life's demands, job demands, relationships, family issues, over packed and unnecessary friendships, haters, doubters, and liars. These all seemingly need to be carried. I see so many people each day over packed and excessed with all the things they honestly think they must carry. You cannot carry them all – that weight will kill you.

Kill your dreams
Kill your passion
Kill your love for life
Kill your desires to grow and glow
Kill the very thing about you that makes you – you!

So today, decide what to carry. Look at all you have to carry and make a decision. Trust me, it seems like you must carry them all, but you do not. The weight of it all will kill you, choose what to carry. If you choose to carry less today, tomorrow you will be alive and well to carry the rest. Wishing you safe travels through this life!

Dr. ABC

Word Power # 5: Emotional Scabs

Can you remember, as a child, how you used to enjoy picking the scab on a cut? (Don't make up your face). I am a school teacher and kids do the same today.

Picking a scab gets many people the attention they need. You pick at it hard enough, it bleeds again, someone has to offer you a Band-Aid and give you hugs and kisses again to make it better.

Wow! With that kind of attention, who would not want to pick a scab?

The issue I am having is that we have many adults who are still picking emotional scabs. They were hurt ages ago and, each and every time, they will go back, pick that scab, allow it to bleed so that they can get the needed attention. We really need to start finding better ways of getting attention.

Why pick that scab? Move on. I do understand that people need time to heal and mourn and recover. I am not talking about that! I am talking about those things you - Yes, YOU, keep going back to resurrect!

That old malice you keep resuscitating.
That old comment your neighbour said about you 10 years ago - keep resurrecting.
That old feeling you had when other people talked bad about you, you keep reviving it.
That old boyfriend or girlfriend who has moved on with their "happily ever after," you keep reincarnating.

That pain you felt when that little boy pushed you when you were 10 - you are now 40! Time to move on! Stop picking that scab.

If you stop picking that scab, I promise you, the pain will go away and who knows, based on the kind of skin you have, the spot will even disappear!

The next time I see you picking that old scab, like my mother would do, I am going slap you on your hand!

Dr. ABC

Word Power # 6: Respect and Appreciate People

As an educational leader and someone who desires to continue to have my future career path in the supervision and development of others, I have learned one very important, simple lesson that I find necessary to share. I looked around at a number of leaders I have worked with in the past and wondered why they have failed to gain the trust, respect and admiration of the people they lead. I could have sought to gain this insight through research and various theories, but great lessons come from our lived experiences. For me, the lesson has been clear and the answer quite simple: RESPECT AND APPRECIATE the people who work for you; those you lead directly.

When you respect people they work harder. When you appreciate and value people, they show up with eagerness and energy. I am sure a salary increase has not been proven to be the number one motivating factor in workplace excellence – indeed it has been recognition.

I have experienced that by letting the cleaner know how much I appreciate my office being so clean, he makes cleaning my office his priority. I have experienced that by letting a teacher know how much I admire the knowledge and skill she brings to her job each day, that teacher pushes more to engage her students. When you respect your subordinates – they will do anything for you. For those of us in positions of authority, don't forget to respect and appreciate those you lead.

Dr. ABC

Word Power #7: Today I am one Day Older and I am Learning

I am learning to invest more in people, just as how I am working hard to secure a monetary pension. I am learning to take the time out of my busy day to do for others what they could not do for themselves. People want to know that you took the time to listen and do for them and it was not rushed and meaningless. I want to ensure I have invested in people, to gain the benefits of a social and emotional pension, when I am old and not as fabulous. Nothing for me is sadder and more fearful than to see a lonely old person. I am learning as I get older, to treat people right, say sorry without thinking if I am being weak. To be vulnerable and human so people can trust me and share with me their time, talent and treasures.

I am learning to say thanks to those people who have helped me on my journey. Those who have offered a smile, a word, a reprimand, a caution, a tissue, a side of their bed, a hug, a cup of tea or whatever – I take nothing for granted and I say thanks. I did not reach here all by myself. I am learning that the best thing you can do with an opportunity is to make full use of it. The best way to show appreciation for a job is to be the best worker. The best way to show that you are grateful for education is to do well in your studies. The best way to say thanks for a gift is to take care of it.

I am learning self-care and self-love. I can't offer love and care to so many who have come to me unless I have loved and cared for myself. I have come to realize I was not made faulty, as I was taught in church, but that God created me fabulous! I am nowhere near perfect but I thank God for making me – me!

I am learning I don't need to always have the last word and I never need to curse or shout to be heard, but speak by my actions. With Facebook, blogs, Twitter etc., words are so common and meaningless these days. Everyone posts a quote and an inspiration - how many of us actually live by them? I am learning to remain authentic – cry when I am hurt and laugh when I am happy. Be truthful to my emotions and allow others to see the honesty in each emotion. Even little children can know when you are pretentious and fake – be real!

I am learning that yes, I am accountable to myself first – but I am still accountable to others.

I am learning that I don't have to always have an answer and it is ok when I don't have the answer. I am not perfect and perfect is over rated. We can't be good at everything. We can't be fabulous all the time. I am learning to look in the mirror and see exactly who God sees. Growing up, I used to see a "sissy" boy, since that is what I was called a lot. Today I look in the mirror and I see a strong, intelligent, hardworking, ambitious, assertive black man. I am a provider and protector. I have come to know that a hard face and rough voice doesn't make you a man, but the level of responsibility and accountability that you carry with grace does. I hope, as you read this teachable moment, you will join me in learning. It is only in learning that we truly grow!

Dr. ABC
(Originally written on my birthday, December 2, 2012)

Word Power # 8: Satisfied

I have been asked about my happiness and why I am happy or what makes me happy. I noted that I have been asked that question a couple times in the past week! I think about my life and the one word that comes to me all the time is SATISFIED. I am happy because I am satisfied. Being satisfied does not mean I am settled. It does not mean that I don't want more, desire more, crave for more and have a passion for more – I do!

It means I am grateful for the now, appreciative of the present and I have stopped to look back and give thanks for the journey so far. If you spend all your waking hours (and some sleeping ones too) thinking, worrying, pacing, pondering, and anticipating about the next move, the next level and the next thing to get – then you never have the time to appreciate your own efforts. I do not have enough and, I'm sure like all of us, I have a wish list of things I would love to have and own. But I cannot afford to be so preoccupied with the things I want, that I forget to be mindful of the things I do have and own.

I have a good time if I am in a 5 star hotel having the best meal ever and I have the same good time if I have to go to McDonalds to grab a meal deal or $1 special. I have enjoyed each steak and lobster and I have enjoyed eating sardines and crackers. So many people work so hard to get everything and in the process they develop anxiety, depression, and ill-health. They cannot enjoy all that they have! Sad, and I mean really sad!

Happiness is an inner feeling. It should not be so over dependent on outside sources. No one can make you happy if you are just a damn sad person! Have you ever seen sad people in happy crowds – happens all the time. You have to come to a place in your life where you are satisfied.

Satisfied with the decisions you made
Satisfied with the chances and risks you took
Satisfied with the mistakes and the lessons learned

Satisfied with who you are, what you have become, the path you have taken, the place you have made home, the people in your life, the friends you own and hold, the partner you have chosen or the one you left.

I am one of the biggest dreamers I know. I have written down my 2 year plan, my 5 year plan and my 10 year plan. I have even made my will. I want to fall in love and live "happily ever after." I have dreams and aspirations and I am bursting each day with anticipation, BUT in all that, I have come to a place where I can stop daily and give thanks to God for the now - I am satisfied.

Dr. ABC

Word Power # 9: Shells are for Peanuts

I spoke with a friend a few weeks ago and asked why I had not seen him as visible as I used to. He informed me of a bad experience he had with someone and because of that he was back in his shell. I guess he thought that being in his shell would keep him safe and protect him from other bad experiences. The first thing that came to my mind was this – you have outgrown your shell!

The experience he had did not kill him but helped in his growth. Going back in a shell would not only stunt his growth but kill his ability to experience life.

A bird breaks out of a shell, and attempts to fly, his wings are not yet developed and he has not gained enough skills to fly on his own. He falls from the nest to the ground and must be taken back. What to do? Of course he does not get to go back into his shell. Instead, he stands at the edge of the nest and attempts the flight again. Soon after, he not only learns to fly, but soars and becomes somewhat of a wonder to us who watch as he takes flight.

Let no one push you into a shell. A shell is your past. You are above a shell – take flight!

Dr. ABC

Word Power # 10: While on Your Way

Today I woke up feeling overwhelmed. I was tired. I had all cylinders going. I got great news about my studies and my PhD defense. I was excited, but immediately I was overwhelmed. There seemed to be so many things that must be done and done now. I needed to respond to emails, get things copied and contact a number of people.

I had a class of 21 great kids that needed my attention. I was teaching online, which I enjoyed and was passionate about. I was hoping and ready to begin dating again, I had some untreated emotional stress to attend to, I was trying to give those around me that needed some attention – some attention.

I still had to be a motivator, the cheerleader, the go-to guy, the leader, the disciplinarian, the lender, uncle, brother, son, and best friend to a number of people. At the same time, I was expected to bathe, cook, eat, breathe, brush my teeth, sleep, drive, walk (yes, no one was assigned to carry me), pray, return phone calls, keep my house clean, not get the flu, keep warm, and shovel snow - I mean real snow! At the same time, I was expected to smile, say thank-you to the cashier at the store, hold the door for that old woman, apologize to that child, answer parents' emails, and respond to students in a kind, inviting voice. All this - just me one!

I needed a hug to be OK. I needed a hug to tell me it would be OK. I needed a hug to say it was OK if it was not OK. I needed a hug to remind me it will be OK. I dragged myself through most of my morning routines and finally got in the car 15 minutes later than my regular departure time. I called one of my best friends for our usual morning drive chat. I shared how I was feeling, and he began sharing his own reasons for also feeling overwhelmed. **Tomorrow was his day to get his open-heart surgery!**

How could I top that! Yes, my stress was no less than his. I also needed my own hugs and encouragement, but when you put them together - the truth is he needed more hugs.

Sometimes we have to remember that in all we are doing there are people out there who need more hugs than we do. Sometimes, God puts those people in our path because he knows we are strong, and we will stand – hugs or no hugs. Do not be so busy and overwhelmed with your own struggles that you do not find time for others. Just this past Sunday in Church, the pastor reminded me that "busy" is a thief of compassion. Jesus was never too busy to stop and attend. Yes, he was always on his way somewhere to do something, but he stopped and allowed the interruptions.

While on his way...He stopped to give the woman at the well the living water

While on his way... He stopped to kneel down to the woman caught in the act of adultery

While on his way.... He stopped to address the woman with the issue of blood

While on his way.... He stopped to heal the sick, raise the dead and even provide wine at a wedding to save the host from embarrassment.

How will you show love and compassion to others while on your way?

Dr. ABC
(Dedicated to a dear friend Kaschka Watson – originally written February, 2014. Today, Kaschka has finished his surgery, doing excellent and he is helping others while on his own way.)

Word Power #11: All the Blue ones should be the Ocean

For years I have watched children put jigsaw puzzles together. I, myself, have not done it much. Once I helped someone put together a 500 piece puzzle and that was indeed a lesson in patience. It was certainly a real challenge. There was, however, one good thing that I figured would help me. The pieces were in colour and I knew that all the blue pieces would make up the ocean. Yes, that would surely help. I was dealing with something familiar and I had some cues to hold on to. Life is not always like that. Sometimes it throws you something that makes the puzzle much more difficult.

What happens when all the blue pieces are not just part of the ocean but now part of the sky?
What happens when what you thought you knew, you were no longer sure of?
What happens when the puzzle of life gives you mixed cues and pushes you to uncertainty?
What happens when you are still not sure if the blue piece you are holding is a piece of the ocean or the sky?

I have watched students complete jigsaw puzzles in impressive record time and I have seen others frustrated to tears. Some would give up and ask to play a different game. There was this one student I had who could never complete the one Dora puzzle I gave her. It only had 25 pieces. She could never get it done. Many of her classmates would just fit it together with such ease. Not her. She was frustrated, hurt and she would give up. "Sir, can I colour?" she would say to me after working hard at it without success. She wanted to go back to just what she could handle. Just what was easy and comfortable.

What puzzles have you given up on?
What puzzles have you left due to shame and embarrassment?
What would you dare not try again since others have convinced you that you are not good enough?

I wish I could tell you it is ok to give up and go colour. It is not. I know the puzzles can be scary and hurtful and intimidating. But you must go back and fit the pieces.

Colouring is easy and beautiful, but it alone will not allow you to grow. You must take on the puzzles – even when all the blue ones are not the ocean.

Dr. ABC

Word Power #12: Keeping-Up

What are you being forced to keep up with today? What is it that you are trying to keep up with? I realize that friendship can sometimes be tested when you are forced to keep up with the group. You should not have to. The truth is, we cannot keep up with everything. We cannot keep up with every event, every party, every date, every fashion, every celebration or even for that matter, every funeral!

It is funny today the assumptions people make about you, when they see your pictures or things you can afford and things you are blessed to enjoy. They know nothing of your history or your decision making process. They fight to keep up or they assume you need to keep up too. The first time I went on a plane I was 21. I can remember how I saved every dollar to make that happen. I lived a few miles from the airport and yet I had never been inside an airport or in a plane until I was 21. I was never a keep up child. From a tender age, I was taught to understand what I had, what I owned and what I did not have, did not own and how to hopefully get it one day. My mother was the kind of mother who taught my siblings and me the realities of our lives and we were happy. She never tried to keep up with others and she taught us not to.

Today it seems that everyone is in a hurry to keep up and many are doing it to their own detriment. You do not need to keep up. I am never trying to keep up with the Joneses; I am way too busy trying to establish the Campbells. That is my advice to you. Focus on establishing you.

Ask yourself where are you going and what your plans are. Are you going in your direction or the direction of the crowd? Are those your plans or the plans established by the crowd? Trying to keep up will only derail your own plans.

Dr. ABC

Word Power # 13: God Kept My Foot from Slipping

In the snow I have to walk gingerly in fear of slipping and falling.
Many people's lives have changed and they live with permanent
injury and pain because their feet slipped.
Many people lose their way because their foot slipped
Many people turn back on the journey because their foot slipped
Many people crashed and died because their foot slipped
People have fallen off cliffs, fallen into pools, fallen into ditches
and ravines, because their foot slipped.
People have lost games because their foot slipped

I have slipped but God caught me
I have slipped but was able to get up
I have slipped but was pulled up by my mother's prayers
I have slipped but was restored by a friend's love
I have slipped but straightened up by God's rebuke
I have slipped but was rescued when God answered no

When your feet slip, one of the first things you do is look around
for something to hold on to, to either break the fall or help you
up.
Do you have friends that you can hold on to?
Do you have family that you can hold on to?
Do you have a living God that you can hold on to?
You just cannot help yourself in all instances. Some people only
trust themselves. You have to trust others.

So, as you walk in this world of puddle, ice, mud, spills --- walk
good.

Dr. ABC

Word Power # 14: Breaking Dishes

I am always a bit mad when I attend a funeral and I see people trying to stop the relatives of the deceased from crying. A funeral is a sad occasion. It is an occasion when we say good bye to those we love. It is a sad moment when a mother buries her child or children lose their parents.

Why are people so scared to express their feelings?
Why do we feel we need to keep it in and fake a smile?
Why do we need to keep it in and pretend we are OK?
Why do we need to keep it in and suffer in silence?

I would hope that at my funeral there is lots of crying. If you miss me, express it - let it out! That is why today we have people who are paid to mourn at funerals. You should have someone who misses you and is angry that you are gone. If not, then we really should write on your head stone *"Good Riddance."*

There are so many of us today who are not honest about our emotions. We are more concerned with what others may think of us if they see us crying or hurting or angry or sad. The truth is, no one is always happy and if you really think that others think you are always happy, then you are actually in a sad state. I am a very happy person - but I know when to have a real good cry and let it out. I know when to break a few dishes and get the anger out. I know when to slam a few doors, walk away from it all, hang up the phone or get out the car. These expressions of hurt and pain are natural. The other day I saw a post from a very good friend of mine. I read it once and raised my eyebrow thinking "wow." Then I read it a second time and I realized that he used the opportunity to let it out! I spoke with him a few days after - sure enough he was doing great. He let it out, cried a bit, cursed a bit, broke a few dishes and today he is better. I am happy he did - I just can't imagine what would have happened if he kept it all in and then decided to let it out one day when he was alone with me - maybe I would make the 6:00 news?

People like people who are real. Real about their feelings. Real about their emotions. Real about what is happening to them.

One of my major concerns is about those people who keep all that anger inside. I am scared of those people. I believe that like a ticking time bomb they will eventually explode! I don't want to be around when they do. We need to let others know it is OK to be upset and angry and let it out. Cry if you must and break some dishes if you must. Rhianna, in one line of one of her songs says, *"I'm breaking dishes up in here, all night. I ain't gon' stop until I see police lights."*

Maybe today you need to break some dishes. Just ensure you break the cheap ones - not your good china!

Dr. ABC

Word Power # 15: Even in the Midst of the Errors

Me: Are you ok?
Six year old girl: Yes Sir, I am just thinking about my life.
Me: Really? Come here, share with me what you thinking.
Six year old girl: I am just thinking how happy I am to be in grade 2 and be in this school. In my country, I did not get to go to kindergarten.

This little girl stopped me in my tracks. She was in my ESL class. She was from a country where they did not have all the freedom that we do enjoy in Canada and oftentimes take for granted. For over twenty years, I have taught little children. The children would write me little notes. At times, they would spell my name wrong, the grammar was wrong, the tense was wrong. They would write "you *are the bestest teacher.*"

If I always took the time to focus on all the grammar and the spelling of my name, then I would miss the message. How often we stop to criticize and correct everything around us and miss out on the blessing.

How many times someone did you a favour and it was not to your "standard" and so you missed out on the message. Has someone ever cooked with love for you but it wasn't quite the right flavour and you missed out on the effort that person put into it?

We cannot correct everything - We cannot fix everything - We cannot make everything right. We cannot have everything perfect - But we can appreciate it all.

Dr. ABC

Word Power # 16: Stay in Your Lane

Each morning, on my way to work, I drive on the 401 (highway) which, at times, can be as many as 6 lanes. There is a skill to driving and overtaking and keeping up on these multi-lane highways. You have to be careful of those in front, those beside and those behind. I have to be mindful of those who will merge and those who will exit. This is a lot to be mindful of when I am just trying to get to where I am going in my own lane.

I know my lane and my lane gets me to work on time. One of the things that works for me is the ability to choose the right lane early and stay in that lane. I am not fascinated with those who are overtaking or those in fabulous sports cars that pass by like a wind going way over the speed limit. I never try to drive as fast as them or show them I can change lanes too just for a show. Too many of us are distracted in life trying to show others we can change lanes, trying to drive in other lanes that carry us in the wrong direction. Too many of us are overtaking unnecessarily and way too many of us do not know the value of staying in our lanes.

Staying in your lane has a negative connotation for many people. I have heard people verbally abuse others and curse at them to stay in their lanes, as to say - stay in your place. That is not my intention. My intention is to remind you to be focused and get to where you need to go in life. There is so much distraction around us and if we forget where we are destined to go and begin to switch lanes, overtake unnecessarily, speed, merge, exit - all without a strategy, then we will find ourselves off the highway and in some gully or ditch somewhere, beaten-up and punctured.

So as you go about today, remember your purpose, your goal and destiny and stay in your lane.

Dr. ABC

Word Power # 17: Home is Where the Heart is

The other day in class I asked my students to share what they did for their long weekend. All the children who went somewhere far and fancy were eager to share and share again. They spoke of the mall, museum, sleep overs, movies, camping, airport, and parties.

A number of students did not share readily. Of course, being the teacher I am, I needed everyone to share their experience and be heard, so I asked them what they did. I noted a disappointing trend - all the students who stayed home said, *"I did nothing, I stayed home."*

So I pushed and I asked what they did at home. Sure enough, they did really exciting and valuable things. They spent time with mom and dad, watched a movie with dad, helped mom with the garden, baked with mom, and all the precious things that offer our children life, love, stability and longevity.

I was bothered! Who taught these children that these things were nothing? What cues have we given to our children so they believe that if they do not go to a party or the mall then they have done nothing! It is sad the number of children we have today that do not know the beauty of sitting in their mom's or dad's lap and just talking, bonding, and getting all the positive attention that they need.

I miss those days when I use to wait for dad to eat so I could get some of his dinner. I was not hungry, I just knew it felt special when I got to eat from my dad's plate and he saved a piece of his meat for me. I really did not care much about the food - I cared for the "daddy time" - I cared for the connections and the opportunities to hear about his day. My dad did not have much to give us, but I still cherish the days he would take my brother and me to the beach in his old taxi car, which oftentimes, we would have to push start. I knew I was special. I got to spend many Saturday mornings like that with my dad.

We are so busy giving our kids things; we forget to give them time. We are so busy taking them places we forget to take them inside our hearts.

Let us invest in our children and families and significant others today. Spend quality time. If we are bored at home all the time - maybe we need to think if we really do have a home.

Dr. ABC

Word Power # 18: Holding Each Other Accountable

For 2014 I plan to hold many of you accountable for your new year's resolutions. It is high time we need to hold each other accountable. So when you say you want to lose weight and I see you eating all kinds of junk, I will tell you to step away and go grab a salad and better yet – run two miles.

When you say you want a new better job, I will ask you on January 30th and every month end until…….how many resumes have you sent out for the month. When you say you want to be a better person, I will ask you what measurable good deeds have you done today or did yesterday.

When you say you want a better education, and I see you watching TV all day and being on FB all day, I will tell you to get your ass off social media and grab a book.

When you say you want to save to buy a car, house, vacation etc., and I see you trying to buy every piece of new clothes they advertise, then I will tell you fashion fades and foolishness stains – put it back on the rack or wait for it to go on sale.

When I see you being mean and hoarding all for yourself, I will remind you that you will reap what you sow – give and it shall be given back to you.

When I see you looking and treating others as if they're nothing – I will remind you of God's mercy towards you, so you can extend the same to others.

When I see you throwing away your dreams because others say you can't, I will remind you of the great people before you who had just what you had.

When you think your life is too messy to get better, then I will remind you of the woman at the well.

When someone makes you feel like you are so wicked and there is no grace for you, then I will remind you of the woman caught in the very act of adultery.

When you break down crying and want to give up and throw in the towel, I will push you, pull you, prop you up or whatever you need to stay on top of the surf and waves.

When you're just plain ole tired- I will bring you water but will require you to get up after the rest. Anything else I cannot do – I will call for Olivia Pope from the ABC hit drama *"Scandal"*
It is high time someone holds you and me accountable!!! I am holding you accountable and you better do the same for me – that is how we will see growth, experience excellence and be better!

Dr. ABC

Word Power # 19: Place Value

This week I am taking my students back through place value. Place value is a topic I used to teach every September. It is the base of many math topics. You cannot really build on higher order concepts unless you truly understand place value. Simply, place value states that every number has a place and every number has a value. If you move a number to another place, it changes its value. For example, in this number 500 - the digit 5 means five hundreds. In this number 105, the digit 5 means 5 ones. 5 ones is a long way off from 500. Yes they are both 5s but based on their place, they have clear differently value.

What place are you sitting in?
What place have you decided to stay in?
Are you planning on moving from that place?
Do you want to increase your value?
Are you happy being in the ones column?
Do you know that you can move from the ones column to the hundreds, and even the millions!!
Just think if that same 5 was here at 5,000,000 – Wow! What a value! What a place to be!

I always smile when I hear others say, "We are all the same" – We are not all the same and I am sure I do not have to honestly show you the differences there are between yourself and many others.

What will you do today to change your place?
What will you do today to change your value?
Let us continue to work hard at moving our place and we will surely see a change in our value.

Dr. ABC

Word Power # 20: Magic with Your Own Hands

Growing up in a relatively poor community in Jamaica, I could see the large homes on the hills from where I lived. As a child we knew that rich people lived in those big houses. They had many rooms, large televisions, beautiful gardens, pools, cars, vacations and lots and lots of things. They had what we were taught as little children to be a success. I always had a desire to live in one of those houses. I wanted exactly what they had - I wanted success.

I grew up at a time when drug dealing was very popular and we would often see another kind of success on TV - big cars, lots of women, - drug dealers.

At that same time many little boys and girls wanted to be a singer or DJ - these young men from the ghetto and inner city of Kingston who had found fame in the dancehall were also showing success - big gold chains, big cars, shiny clothes, lots of travelling, lots of women - Kings of the Dancehall.

How could I be successful?
How could I get on the hill?
How could I travel and take vacations?
How would I own these things and have that success?
What would it take?
What was I willing to do?

I knew from early on that I would not be a DJ - I know my limits. I also knew I could not sell drugs - I have too much of a conscience and once a police man was within 100 feet; I knew I would sweat like a pig - I was not built for that. I could not go to jail. I also knew I could not be a prostitute. No one I knew was buying young black boys and I had no role models there - I am happy I did not even try that path! The only thing I knew was to work with my hands. I knew I would be able to make magic with my own hands.

Today with the magic in my hands, I have moved from not enough, to just about enough to now having a little more than enough.

Today with the magic in my hands, I have moved from having to struggle to pay my school fees back at Mico Teachers College and Jamaican Theological Seminary to now having a PhD paid in full by myself.

Today with the magic in my hands, I have worked hard at my jobs and I am able to afford so many of those things I figured meant success.

We must teach our children the power of the magic in their own hands. What it is to work hard for the things they desire.

What it is to make use of educational opportunities. What it is to try a business idea. What it is to begin somewhere and work hard towards an intended goal. The next time your child or anyone comes to you and shares their own desire to live on the hill - ensure you point out to the magic in their hands. Abracadabra! – It's in you!

Dr. ABC

Word Power # 21: Get Real

I honestly think there are far more fake people around today than 30 years ago, when I was much younger. These people are not necessarily fake to others – the danger is that they are fake to their own selves. Thirty years ago, as children, we used to play real games, have real friends, and had real fights with those friends. We ate real food cooked by our real moms (dads, aunties or grandparents) and then we drank real lemonade made with fresh limes from a real tree in some neighbour's yard. We would do real homework and then drink some real tea before saying a real prayer and heading off to bed.

Today, not many people care about being real. Ladies wake up, often times not out of their real (own) beds. They put on a fake wig, enough make up to cover the fakeness and hurt and big red lipstick they hope will cover their pain and loneliness. They have fake breasts, fake butt, fake hips, and are all dressed up in fake (faux) fur. They did not stop to eat breakfast since they just need to have coffee with creamer (not real fresh milk) and sweetener (not real sugarcane sugar) with that, they have a muffin with no calories (really??) and then egg whites only (I guess they will soon have a hen that can lay eggs without yolks?). They like fat free (fake) bacon and non-diary cheese (I thought cheese should come from a real cow or goat?)

They jump into their cars; say hi to the many pretend friends they have on Facebook and then off to a job that they pretend to like. They pretend to be productive all day and then head back home to a partner that they pretend to love. They see you later that evening and they pretend to be excited, offer a fake smile and engage you in a fairy tale conversation. They keep the real things in, and so, they can't afford to have a real laugh or shed a real tear. Are you real with you? If not – it is time to get real!

Dr. ABC

Word Power # 22: It is OK to be Human

When you are a role model or a motivator for others, sometimes you forget that it is ok to be human. We forget that real people appreciate and crave real role models. Because we have to be "ON" so much, we forget that it is natural for us to be "OFF" sometimes. No one in this world can be "ON" all the time – no one! No matter how much you smile, no matter how fabulous you look, no matter how much money you have - it is just not possible or natural. Even Superman takes off his "S" sometimes. I do believe Batman and Wonder Woman do the same.

The other day I felt a bit overwhelmed with my "to do" list. I spoke with one of my best pals and I told him how overwhelmed I was feeling. I had kept it in for two whole days. Immediately I felt such a release as I reminded myself it is OK to have this feeling. It is OK for me not to feel like laughing or smiling or talking. It is OK for me not to feel like I have to say yes to every request, or answer every phone call or rush to reply to every email or text message. Overwhelmed is a place – a real place. It is fine to visit that place BUT don't live there! Don't give yourself another excuse to be down or stressed or depressed, but in the same breathe be real about how you feel. Step one is always being honest with yourself. It is OK to be human, even for a while.

Dr. ABC

Word Power # 23: Don't Let Anyone Steal Your Applause

Oftentimes, people see you and they look at you and make judgments. They have a problem with you climbing, growing and being next in line. They have a problem with you loving who you are and wanting to be the best. These are the people who try to steal your applause. They think you are too much and think too much of yourself. They look at you and wonder why you are here and how the hell did you get here. I stopped today from my busy schedule to ask those people a question. Where were you?

Where were you when I could not to go 6th form with my friends because my mom could not afford it and I had to start working full time at 16?
Where were you when I cried because my mom was sending me to credit groceries from Mr. Wray's shop again and she did not yet pay the last bill?
Where were you when I owed Jamaica Theological Seminary so much school fees that they wrote me a letter reminding me not to return if I didn't pay for my studies?
Where were you when I taught a class of 45 ten year olds all day, took two buses into town to attend evening studies for 3 hours, and then took two buses back home - fell asleep many nights and passed my stop?
Where were you when I had to wear the clothes my brother outgrew? Thank God I finally grew taller than him!
Where were you, when as a child I thought peanut butter, KFC and Burger King were considered rich people food?
Where were you when my friends would tell me about their travels and I thought I would never get to go on a plane?
Where were you when I cried at the of age 25 the first time I saw my name on a birthday cake?

These are the same people who come and see you near the front of the line in life and have an issue. They wonder how you got to the front of the line or how you even got in this line at all.
They wonder how you got in this line with your coloured skin

They wonder how you got in this line and you did not live on the hill.
They wonder how you got in this line and your parents were poor.
They wonder how you got in this line and you seem gay for sure.
They wonder how you got in this line and you are not married or have kids.

Well the answer is simple. I joined the line years ago at the back like everyone else, and with God's keeping grace and mercy, worked very hard, and waited in line through many circumstances.

If you have ever waited in any line you will know the feeling. So wait in line and you too will get near the front. Let no one allow you to feel like you should not be in that line. The next time someone looks and tries to make you feel that you think too much of yourself, look at them and ask them, "Where were you?" and then wait for 30 seconds and then say, " You won't steal my applause."

Dr. ABC

Word Power # 24: Hold the Mirror for Me

Have you ever seen people on the street and you wondered to yourself if they own a mirror. Why did they leave the house like that or was someone else at home to correct or admonish them not to leave the house in that state? I have lived alone for years and I know the disadvantages of having to put on my own cuff links, fix a bow-tie or check the back of my head. I know what it is like to leave the house, thinking I am well-dressed, only to have someone point out a mistake.

It is shocking to know the number of people who cannot tell their friends what they see. A friend is a safe critic. Many of us forget the usefulness and value of a real friend. One of the many purposes of that friend is the ability to hold the mirror for you - help you to see exactly what is happening, where you may not be able to see clearly. I am not talking about the kind of fairytale friends you have where they think you are just always fabulous and everything is always pretty, pink and full of colour and sparkles like a bag of Skittles. I am also not talking about the kind of pretend friends you have where you know their words will cut you, damage you, or destroy you. I am not even sure why you would have someone that you are so fearful of their words as a friend. No matter how much you look into the mirror, we often times see a different picture. That picture is blurred because of our perception of ourselves or our lived experiences.

I call a lot of people friends and of course there are degrees and levels to friendship. The mirror holders for me are those that are very close, my inner circle, the ones who have seen me at not just my best, but at my worst. The ones who I can honestly tell when I am not feeling as fabulous as you may think and they take nothing away from me the next time I walk into a room and claim "fabulosity." That is a mirror holder!

I have run to my friend about something that has happened in my relationship, knowing for sure that he would agree with my actions, only to have him look me in the eye and say "You were wrong" – mirror holder!

I have run to my friend to let him know my boss is the devil and I need to leave this job now or I will kill somebody and he looked at me and said, "So when you walk off this job, how will you pay the rent and take care of yourself?" – mirror holder!

I have run to my friend and cried of the hurt I endured at the hands of other friends and swore never to speak to them again and he looked at me and said, " Well you know you are not very good at keeping malice" – mirror holder!

We need mirror holders to show us where a spot is. We need mirror holders to show us where we missed a button. We need mirror holders to ensure we got the hook. We need mirror holders to check our backs. We need mirror holders to tell us if the zip is inside-out, wrong side up or just plain twisted. As you get dressed for this world, make sure you are able to call that mirror holder and ask them from your heart, "How do I look?"

Dr. ABC
(Dedicated to one of my best friends, Damian Crawford, who has been holding the mirror for me for over 15 years.)

Word Power # 25: It Should Not Have to be a Bargain

The last time I went shopping with my mom was last year in August. She was visiting and we wanted to ensure we got really good bargains for her. I also got some great bargains for myself. You know when you get a real bargain, especially when you have been watching an item for a while and you can actually compare the cost to what you saw months ago. You can calculate the bargain for yourself. You are very clear of what value it has and what you paid for it.

While I was shopping, it dawned on me that things go out of fashion so quickly, seasons change and new styles appear and soon what you have and cherish becomes old and outdated. What was the "must have" item last month is now discounted and placed in the bargain bin this month. People try them on in the dressing room and discard them so easily if they don't fit, not the right color, buttons too big or some other fleeting reason. Material things move from hand to hand so quickly these days. They are reduced, discounted, returned, exchanged, placed on sale, two for the price of one, buy one get the other at ½ price, and return within 30 days if it doesn't fit. I felt this sadness, hurry and waste around me as I watched the stores, sales, and shopping.

How many of these people have treated people in their lives as a new product?
Who have you discounted or reduced?
Who have you returned or exchanged?
Who does not fit you anymore?
What friends have you gotten at ½ price?
I hope we treat the people in our lives, not as some brief must have fashion, but as a timeless piece! vintage! heirloom! – A real bargain! I am keeping my precious pieces near to me, what about you?

Dr. ABC

Word Power # 26: Handle with Care

As a little boy growing up I used to play dolly house a lot. There were two set of girls I played with. One set had old dolls with an eye missing; a leg missing or that had no hair. We would often take out their hands and legs. These dolls would be thrown anywhere and we would do just about anything with these dolls. As a matter of fact these dolls did not even have names. I can't remember ever giving them a name. They were just dolls!

The other set of girls had really nice dolls - Barbies to be exact. They were not just any Barbie, these dolls came from the USA or Canada and they came in the usual Christmas barrels sent by parents and relatives. These were special and, as a matter of fact, they even had names. Each time we played doll house, these dolls had a birthday and we made a very nice cake of mud, decorated with hibiscus flowers. We celebrated these dolls. We cared for these dolls. We were proud of these dolls. We showed off these dolls. We were very careful how we combed their hair, we bathed them all the time, we made real clothes for them and no one - and I mean no one, was allowed to pull out their hands or legs! There was a clear understanding of the difference with the dolls and how we handled them.

Many of us settle for the bad care that we receive because we feel like we are at that desperate place or last resort spot. You are scared of losing what you have. You don't wish to be single. You are getting too old to be single. What will your friends think if you are single? Have you failed yet again? If these are your many questions, then I have another question for you - Are you happy? Is this all you want?

We must reach the point with all our relationships – family, friendship, professional and intimate, where we can tell others how to handle us.

Do you feel like you have been handled with care?
How are you being treated in your relationship?

Are the persons in your life pulling out your hands and legs?
Is your hair being combed?
Do the ones who profess their love for you, make you clothes?
Do they celebrate you!
Do they call you by your name and give you the attention you deserve?
Have you settled for not having a name, not being thrown a party, not being given a bath and only getting to be played with when the better dolls are not available?
Do you allow others to pull out your hands and legs?

Have you just given up on the desire to be happy and settled in because this has now become your reality and new normal?
Have you decided not to ruffle the feathers in asking for better or demanding more?
I shop online a lot. I can tell what is in a box by the very packaging. Not everything can be thrown into a box, sealed and posted. There are things that must be handled with care.
There are things you must send with a sign "fragile".
There are things that must be sent through overnight courier service since they are urgent.

There are things that are so precious that they won't send them unless you pay for insurance.
There are things that are so essential that someone must be home to sign for the package.
There are things that are so confidential that they ask that only the person to whom it is addressed can receive the package.
What is in your package?
How should it be handled?
Have you thought of letting those in your life know how you wish to be handled?
Are you hurting because you are not being handled with care by the ones you love?
Don't you think it is full time that you are handled with care?

Dr. ABC

Word Power # 27: Find the Value

How many times have you seen something old and you think of it as having no value? Many people have to call in appraisers today to determine the value of things they own. They do not use them, they occupy space and they are not really sure of their value.
How much do you value the friends in your life?
How much do you value your family and loved ones?
How much do you value your job? (Yes that job that you curse at everyday which pays the mortgage, the rent, buys the clothes and food and keeps you independent or at least above the poverty line.) How much do you value the people who have helped you along the way? Maybe we should really do some appraising today. If something is of value - keep it, shine it, use it and ensure that you make that value known to others. If that something or someone is not of the value you think it was worth - do away with it. Nothing is wrong with giving away things and people in our lives that add no value. You would be shocked how valuable that thing or person is for someone else.

A couple months after I came to Canada in June 2008, I moved into a little apartment at the side of a house. Well it was not really an apartment, it was a garage turned into a studio apartment. I was just starting over and needed some help. My niece gave me a big box TV she had in storage. She had other TVs, flat screen and fabulous. This TV was no longer as valuable to her. I was happy to have it. It was placed in my bedroom and for two years I watched that big 19" box TV. It was valuable to me!
What you consider old - may just be antique.
What you consider out of style - may just be vintage.
What you consider useless - may just be what someone else needs to make them happy.
Stop to count your blessings today. Do some appraising today - I bet you, you will find higher value in the things and people around you.

Dr. ABC

Word Power # 28: Gossip the Gospel

Gossip is sweet! It is exciting, juicy and most of all it is not about us. It is funny how much joy many of us take in hearing the bad news about others. Who wants to hear that someone got a new job, was promoted, graduated, had a baby, got married, bought a new car - who wants to hear all that boring stuff? Forget it, give me the juice, and share with me the mess and the dirt. That is what makes good TV and a good news story.
Yes, we want to hear the juicy stuff. We want to hear that someone was beaten by their husband, they lost their job, their child is on drugs, their brother committed suicide, and they slept with their best friend's boyfriend. These things are front page news these days. Gossip sells? Bad news is good news!

If we are honest, we can say it is easy to gossip. It takes no real skill, you don't need any qualifications, you don't need to attend school, you don't have to arrive anywhere on time, you don't need to bathe and get dressed. All you really need is a good story that is not really proven and a dirty set of ears that are willing to listen - and just like that, you have created a good, nice piece of gossip! Just like that you are a qualified *Gossipologist*!

Today, I would love for you to try something else. Try gossiping the gospel. The gospel is simply defined as the "good news of Jesus." Today, I am going to take the liberty and borrow the word for a bit and adjust the meaning. For the purpose of this chat, we will define gospel as simply "good news." So here is my homework for you.

I want everyone to take a few minutes today and gossip the gospel about someone. Be very serious about it. Call up someone, who also knows that someone, who you know, knows something about that someone. Make sure you don't tell that someone what I told you to say about that other someone. Ensure that as you tell that someone about the other someone, that someone is really into hearing about the other someone. Wow - you see how messy even the homework about gossip can sound?

If that someone is in your physical presence - I want you to go in for the kill when you share the gossip. I mean, I want you to pull them aside in a corner, raise your eyebrow, widen your eyes, tilt your head to the side, intersperse the stories with ohhhs, ahhhs , yes girl!! and yes sir!!!Give them the whole juicy story - do not hold back!

Call someone and tell them something really good (the gospel) about someone else. Make sure you add all the usual juice and spice. None of us is perfect and none of us is above this homework.

Isn't it full time we all get A+ when we talk about others?

Dr. ABC

Word Power # 29: Everyone Cannot be a Star, But Everyone Can Shine

I was speaking to a teacher about our students and the importance for me, as a teacher, to have all my students grow and learn during the time they are with me. I am not that teacher who thinks every child deserves a star or a sticker - I believe that they need to work for that and be given the opportunity to excel. Too often, we reward people for little or no effort. When we do this, we limit their potential to grow and shine. However, if you ask many of my past students what is one word that they can remember I always use in reference to them, they would say "star."

I am of the belief that everyone can shine and should shine. The issue is that many of our children and even adults need someone to bring out that shine. I think, at times, we forget that there are people who for some honest reason or the other, cannot shine on their own - your job, whether you like it or not is to bring out that shine in them.

I like silver a whole lot. I must confess that I do not spend the time to shine it as much as I should. I own a number of pieces and I wear them very often. Once in a while, when someone cleans them for me or when I take them to the jewelry store to be cleaned, I am always excited at how brightly they shine. I sometimes forget that these same pieces are mine and they are the ones I have been wearing for months. After a real clean, they are noticed. After a real clean, people value them. After a real clean, they sparkle and shine. Nothing beats a shine!

The next time you look at someone and you think they will never be a star- dull or lacking, just remember that you are possibly the one that is placed there to bring out their shine. Not everyone can be a star, but everyone can shine.

Dr. ABC

Word Power # 30: Tell What It Takes

Too often, we only see someone at the end of a journey and we celebrate with them. We are happy to celebrate their new car, new house, completing a degree, or a successful surgery. How often do we see someone in a magazine or on stage and we think to ourselves, I would really like to look like that person. Well, I am sure you know they did not get to look like that by sitting down and eating anything they felt like at anytime and anywhere. There is an effort and a discipline to that. What we forget is to share with others what it takes to get there. Why is this important? Far too often, those who wish to walk in those same shoes are not aware of the real facts. Why do we refuse to share the process and the journey? - everyone knows that things don't just happen. There is a process.

We refuse to share the time when we were in college and things were so bad that we wondered if we had made the right decision - but now we have many degrees.

We refuse to share the times when things were so bad and it was our best friend, who had just as little, who shared with us - but now we can buy and afford all of what we need and most of what we want.

We refuse to talk about the many times we have taken the one pair of shoes we had to the shoe repair - but now we own a closet full of shoes.

We refuse to talk about the many days we had to eat what was provided and what was provided was the only thing in the house - but now we can go to any restaurant and order anything on the menu.

When we refuse to share all these, then we rob those watching us of the authentic opportunity to be all that they can be. When I was an administrator at Everest College, I used to always remind the students that if everyone could just get up and get a diploma, then there would have been no need for a college, teachers, paying tuition, buying books, doing homework, studying, and attending placement - success takes work and effort!

I find in talking to many people, that they often have no idea what it takes to get where they need to be. The sad thing is that many of us could help more people, inspire more people, and motivate more people, if we just tell them what it takes. The next time someone comes to you and offers all the praise and adulation and wants to be just like you, help them to get there, tell them what it takes.

Dr. ABC

Word Power # 31: Who Gets the Glory? (A Prayer)

I pray to God that you will provide jobs for my friends and family who are seeking jobs. Not just any job, but a desired job, a job that they have studied or trained or equipped themselves for. Blow your mighty wind on those resumes and frustrate the spirit of disappointment and bring their applications to the top. Throw favour in their path so that they can receive the unexpected. Surprise them with substance and satisfy them with soundness.

I pray for those who are sick in mind that you will whisper peace. Those who are troubled and hurting emotionally and don't have access to a "listener", I pray Lord that you speak inner peace. You go into their lonely space, like I know you can, and show yourself merciful. Teach them how to smile from within and give them back a song. Teach them how to handle this unforgiving world and how to push against the wind.

I pray for those of us who are too fabulous to recognize when we are failing and faulty. I pray that we recognize when we are faulty so that we can be rushed to mending. Like a bad cut, undressed and ignored, we can turn into a sore. I pray that we will take responsibility for our faultiness and seek mending quickly. No one likes to be classified as faulty, but help us to step away from pride and seek urgent mending. A cut needs a Band-Aid – a sore needs a bandage.

I pray for those who are weak and tired and too tired to even be tired. I pray for those who are tired of trying. Many are feeling like the fishermen who left that seaside tired and disappointed. You spoke to them to cast their net once more. I, myself, am not sure if I would have cast my net again. Being trained fishermen, they must have questioned your knowledge of the sea and the craft of fishing. But nevertheless at your word, they cast their nets and what a result! Many of us are hindered by our own training and intelligence. We are so well thought-out that we forget to trust. I pray that you will teach us how to ignore our own abilities and talents and knowledge when needed and trust in you. Help us to know when our PhDs and MBAs and BAs are not enough for the journey and help us to trust you, the master teacher!

I pray especially for those who are feeling pushed aside and excluded. I pray for those who are feeling alone and left out. I pray for those who are feeling little in a big country. Remind them:

You are still that neighbour - you are that neighbour that speaks over the fence.
You are that neighbour that shares a meal.
You are that neighbour that calls each morning to ensure they made it through the night.
You are that neighbour who lends salt to flavour, and pepper to taste.

Dr. ABC

Word Power # 32: The Sun Actually Comes Out

Just this past winter, while on a road trip, I came across really heavy fog. I could not see more than 15 feet in front of the car. This was on a highway and it was my first time driving in such conditions. The fog was so thick I had to decide what to do and quick. I thought to myself, it is 4 a.m., maybe I left too early and should have waited until the sun rose or maybe I should just pull over and wait it out. Of course I was even a bit scared. I decided to break my speed and use every resource I had in the car to navigate through it. After 30 minutes of heat regulation, windshield usage, and speed regulation I came out to the most beautiful sunrise coming from way behind the mountains.
In life sometimes the fog will block your destined journey so much that you fear for your very life!!

Should you stop?
Should you give up?
Should you turn back?
Should you just pull over and quit?

Here is what you do ---use all your resources and continue to navigate this thing we call life. Stay on your path. Keep to the itinerary. Cut speed if you must but stay on the road!!!
THE SUN COMES OUT!!!

Dr. ABC

Word Power # 33: Standing Alone

When you stand for a cause, be prepared oftentimes to know you will stand alone. You will wonder why others around you are not fighting too. You wonder why others are not speaking out against the injustice and prejudice that you see. But it is not their fight, it is yours.

It takes guts and courage to stand alone in the face of adversity. When you stand against such things as racism, discrimination and homophobia, be prepared to stand alone. Think back on all the heroes you know both real and make believe – they stood alone.

Moses stood up to Pharaoh, David to Goliath and Paul to the Galatians. There is no such thing as supermen, batmen, or wonder women. NO, these are all singular -Superman, Batman, and Wonder Woman. Greatness comes with a price and there is a cost for a cause. Ask Martin Luther King Jr., ask Rosa Parks, and ask Marcus Garvey.

So next time you feel alone in your fight and your cause, be reminded that standing up for a cause will be a lonely road at times – stand anyhow!

Dr. ABC

Word Power # 34: In a Competition with Yourself

So many people feel like they have failed since they are constantly in a competition with others. They measure their successes and failures based on others. This is actually not wrong since we do live in a world with others and we are constantly being judged against others by others.

In the words of one of the most famous poets,
"If you compare yourself with others,
you may become vain or bitter, for always
there will be greater and lesser persons than yourself"
(Desiderata, 1927 Max Ehrmann)

In the words of one of my favourite singers of all time:
"I decided long ago, never to walk in anyone's shadows.
If I fail, if I succeed, at least, I'll live as I believe"
(Greatest Love of All, Whitney Houston)

I would encourage those of you who may be struggling to try something different - enter a competition with yourself.
Sign up the entry forms by yourself
Exercise and prepare by yourself
Get ready to be on the track by yourself
You must win!
There is no one else running but you, so when you arrive at the finish line, that is the official time for the race to be completed.
There is no one who has set a record for you so the time you clock (in) will be your personal best.
There is no one to pass you a baton so you can't drop the baton.
There is no one else in the race so you can't run out of your lane.
Take this opportunity to start a competition with YOURSELF.
Just imagine the feeling when you complete the race, clock in the best time, get your trophy and celebrate.

Dr. ABC

Word Power # 35: What a Difference a Day Makes

New day. New mercies. New opportunities. New chances. New takes. New learning. What a difference a day makes!!!!
I have had those days when I regretted waking up!
I knew it would be a bad day.
I was not ready to face what was to come and I wished I could have skipped that day.

BUT!

We don't get to skip those days
We don't get to sleep until they are past
We don't get to trade in those days for better days

INSTEAD!

What we get is to face those days
What we get is to realize that there is more in us than we thought or imagined
What we get is to realize that no matter how long, sorrows never last forever
What we get is an opportunity to show what is truly inside us, and what we are made of
What we get is facing the day, its challenges and growing from them
What we get is to fail and understand the meaning behind our failures so that we know how to equip ourselves for the next challenge
What we get is to realize how imperfect we are and that our human strength has limitations to enable us to connect to a higher source
What we get is to flex our inner muscles and inner super powers to give us the strength to walk away with a wow moment that we did it!

If we sleep through all the days of woes, then we will never get the days of wonder.

If we sleep through the days of fights, then we will never get the days of fame.

If we sleep through the days of despair, then we will never get those days of distinction.

New day. New mercies. New opportunities. New chances. New takes. New learning. What a difference a day makes!

Dr. ABC

Word Power # 36: Haters Who?

Each time I sign into Facebook or listen in on some stranger's conversation on the bus or subway, there is always someone sending a message to his/her haters! Why take all this time and effort to be sending them messages? Why invest all this emotion in what they think about you? I know it takes a level of maturity that many of us do not yet possess, but we have to grow fast to last, and this is one area I implore us all to grow in and grow quickly.

The best way to deal with haters is to be successful. I laugh at many people who are sending messages to their haters, but are making no real changes to the very thing that haters want to see happen to them. Again, I say, the best way to deal with haters is to be successful at everything that they hope you will fail at. In other words, disappoint them!

You disappoint them not with words of hate and violence, but with your growth, success and accomplishments. You disappoint them, not with malice and envy, but with a smile and a kind word. (Yes, it is hard to offer a kind word. Trust me. I know. But the feelings you get afterwards are priceless. Hesitate no more but try it!)

Do not give any hater much attention and time. I am one who is not good at keeping inside what I am thinking or feeling. If you hang around me long enough, you will be sure if I like you or not. It takes really too much energy and effort to be fake and pretentious. But I have grown to realize that when we give haters so much time and energy, they grow and we grieve. They blossom and we fade. They strive and we become stagnant.

The next time someone wants to engage you in talking about your haters, just say to them - who?

Dr. ABC

Word Power # 37: Courtesy or Crookedness?

Why do people do things they believe they are doing out of courtesy and then it never ends up with a good after taste? We all make resolutions we don't keep. After much inner-man-check and self-rebuke, almost a year now, I made a promise and intend to keep it until death. Here goes:

Never attend a funeral if you're really not willing to pay your last respect. What is the use of paying last respect at death to someone you never even liked in life?
Never attend a wedding if you truly don't wish the couple the best. Why waste your money to buy new clothes and purchase gifts for people you don't care about?
Never sit and have a meal with people you don't truly want to be around. This is the easiest way to get an upset stomach and even an ulcer!
Never sit beside someone you can't stand - even if it is the last seat. Stand for the time. It will develop your posture.
Don't offer people things when you are praying on the inside that they would say no to your offer. Really?
Never wear clothes you feel uncomfortable in. Feeling like a fool is worse than looking like a fool. What lady Gaga has is confidence. Leave fashion and get style.
Don't buy gifts for people just because they gave you one. Giving is not about an exchange. Who wants a gift that was forced anyhow?
When you are invited somewhere and you don't want to attend, send your regrets and live your truth. In doing so you have been better to those people than if you were present.

So the next time you pull one of these stunts - ask yourself, am I being courteous or crooked?

Dr. ABC

Word Power # 38: Leave Satan Alone

Growing up everything bad that happened to us, we were taught to blame the devil. Of course he deserves all the blame – he is wicked and terrible and is no good! However, I am concerned that many of us have blamed the devil and used him as a scape-goat for our own misdeeds.

We spend our hard earned money in very silly ways, buy what we don't need, go where we don't need to be and try to keep up with others and when we are broke, we say that the devil is stealing our blessings.

We go to work late, do not do enough, text all day, take extra lunch time and when we are fired we blame the devil.
We choose the wrong partners - allow them to use and abuse us and then we blame the devil.

We decide to study - but spend more time on TV, on Facebook, in the malls, in bed and then when we fail, we blame the devil.

We are not nice to people - we don't treat our neighbours right and then we say they are the devil.

It is so good to not have to be able to take responsibility and accountability for our actions. It is so sweet to just say the man in the red body tights, pitch fork, long tail and horns, who lives underground in fire did it!

Yes, yes and a thousand times yes! - The devil is wicked and terrible but do not use him as a scapegoat for ALL failures. When you do that, then you take away the responsibility and accountability from yourself. The next time we think of something that is going wrong in our lives - stop and think. The devil did it or did I cause that?
"Get behind me Satan!"

Dr. ABC

Word Power # 39: Celebrate You

Today I went out to the supermarket, got me a cake, candles, came back home and had a celebration. It was not my birthday, it was not my anniversary and it was not any regular calendar occasion - I just felt to celebrate ME!

I am not all about self, and if you know me well, you will know I am very big on celebrating others and I am all about people. However:

It is important that I know how to master my own celebrations, It is important that I know how to appreciate me, It is important that I know how to encourage me, motivate me, inspire me, push me, lift me up and cheer me on, It is important that I celebrate me.

Take some time today to celebrate you:
Take you out for dinner - just you and you,
Take you out to see a movie - a big bag of popcorn just for you,
Open that special bottle of your favorite wine you have been keeping for so long and have a drink with you,
Cook you something special and set the table for one,
Take a walk by the park and share some thoughts with you,
Buy a bunch of roses and place them on your desk at work - yes, let the others know it is from you to you
Watch how much you appreciate others as you learn to appreciate yourself more!!!

Dr. ABC

Word Power # 40: Live While You Are Alive

A few years ago a colleague I had taught with for a number of years passed away. She always talked to me about their dream home she was building back in Jamaica. Whenever we had some free time we would talk and her focus was always on that dream house she was building. She was not very happy with the present and always had the yearning for the future. I always encouraged her to live a little now and be happier and connected with the present. She never got to live in the dream house – she died.
It is very important to have your dreams and push for them and invest in getting them. It is equally important that we live in the now, appreciate the now, enjoy the now, and experience the now. While you work and wait for your dream home, make the best of where you lay your head now, while you hope for the dream job, do your best at the one you have now. While you pray for the dream lover, spouse or family, appreciate the ones that are in your life now. You never know when it will be your time to leave this world, so live while you are alive!

Dr. ABC

Word Power # 41: Muddy Hands

When someone tells you something bad about someone else, take the time to get your own impression. You would be shocked to know that person is a different person from the one you were told. People respond to people differently, and you should never make someone else's perception of another be your own conclusion.

I have seen where someone who is a bitch to others has been the sweetest person to me. Sometimes the bitchy action of that person to others is a simple response to what they have gotten from them. Take the time to know and learn people for yourself. I have come to realize that there are people out there who are very malicious, and you would burst a vein if you knew the things they have said to others about you! Let no one encourage you to throw mud at others.

Muddy hands throw mud! - go wash your hands!

Dr. ABC

Word Power # 42: Keep Moving

Have you ever been at a crossroad in your life when you honestly, genuinely, do not know which way to go? There is so much confusion, mistrust, doubt, fear, anxiety around you and your decision making process. You have been through it and you just cannot take anymore. Life has again dealt you a bad hand. You are again at a crossroad and you are again flooded with those questions:

What will they say if I do this?
What will they say if they see me doing this?
Do I have the strength in me to do this?
I have tried many other ideas before, should I try this?
Do you think they will laugh at me or say I have failed?

I know the feeling. You wish you could just:
Stop
Park
Shut off your engine
Take a break
Think it out
Take as much time as you need
And then and only then you will keep moving

I hate to be the one to push you again or spoil your moment, but that is not how a crossroad works! Most crosswords are 4-way stops or all-way stops. Everyone must stop, but then everyone must go when they are next. There is no waiting, no keeping up traffic, no trying to call the traffic police, no depending on stop lights, no wishing for crossing guards. You must watch the traffic, be aware when you have arrived at the crossroad and be prepared to move when you are next.

I know only too well that this world is rough and things and circumstances are happening in your life that impact your very being. Sometimes these very circumstances make you question your value, question your purpose, question your existence and question your very dreams. The truth is, you will need to move from that crossroad. You cannot stand there. You will be ticketed. Today, if you are at a crossroad – take courage and keep moving.

Pray for strength and keep moving
Ask your friends for help and keep moving
Reach out to family and keep moving
Cry yourself a river and keep moving
Be angry for a while and keep moving
Remove yourself from the haste of the traffic around you
Talk it over with a confidant or seek professional help and keep moving
Talk to God, share your fears with Him, hide in Him and keep moving
Keep .... Moving.....Keep .... Moving...

Dr. ABC
(Dedicated to a very dear friend – Carlson – just keep moving!)

Word Power # 43: You Don't Have To Win - But You Must Fight

It seems like there is so much bad news and fear and anxiety surrounding the last few weeks. If the truth be told, we all have that level of fear of tomorrow. Only God knows what I would do if I did not have a job tomorrow! But I encourage you all, instead of living in the fear of the times, seriously sit down and count all the blessings. Count especially the ones that money cannot buy and I promise you will feel refreshed.

Too often our lives and all our ambitions are rested on things. Of course we need things and yes, we need money to get those things. Things that make us comfortable and happy. But how many of those things, if denied, will leave you desperate and depressed?

I heard a young man, far too young, say "I just want to lie down and die." That hurt me. It hurt me that at such a young age he felt like the answer to life's challenges is to die. To give up. To give up his fight. I know oftentimes it seems you may be in a constant fight and struggle with life, the challenges in getting to your dream, reaching the next level. There are even fights within family and loved ones and friendship. But something came home to me strongly this morning as I meditated - the title of champion is only given to those who fought.
So fight on.....

Fight on for what it is that you desire
Fight on for what it is you deserve
Fight on for your love and your marriage and your relationships
Fight on to be the best at work and get that top spot
Fight on when others think you should give up
Fight on for those dreams that no one believes can happen to you
Fight on when no one understands your fight
Fight on when you yourself question why bother to fight
Fight on for your sanity

Sometimes you will come to a place when there is no fight left in you. That is when you ensure you have surrounded yourself with good people who will help in your fight. They may not get in the ring on your behalf but they will be there to at least cheer you on. So today, if you are in a fight – fight on! And if you are not in a fight - thank God for being at such a place and cheer on somebody else!!!

Dr. ABC

Word Power # 44: Such as I have, Give I thee

How many of you keep expecting certain actions from your friends, family or partners and you never see it happen? Day after day your expectations are not realized. Day after day you are disappointed by their actions or inactions. Has it ever occurred to you that they may really mean no harm – they just don't have it?

They don't possess the passion
The intimacy you desire
The love you require
The attention you yearn
The commitment you covet
The honesty and truth you revere
They just don't have it!

You have someone who keeps lying to you and you want them to stop. Maybe they just have no truth in them. Come to grips. They are full of lies and if they are full of lies then you will only get lies. A new one next week, another next month and many more to come next year – they give you lies because they have lots of lies to give.

I talked to one of my best friends last year and I expressed how I felt about a number of people who come into my life and just take. And I said I need to give less, offer less and share less. But then as I reflected I said to myself, how can I give less when God has given me so much?

I can't give less love when God has given me so much love
I can't give less honesty, when I have worked and nurtured the truth in me
I can't give less attention, when I believe in the value of time and attention
I keep giving, because it is me. I remember the words of Paul to the man at the Gate "Beautiful such as I have, give I thee." We can only give what we have.

I also look at the other side of the coin. The reason why I may not have gotten from those people is because they just have nothing to give

They have no advice
They have no kindness
They have no love
They have no kind words
They have no hugs, no cheers, no pity, no smiles, no... no...

And like I said before "such as I have, given me thee"
What do you have to give?

Dr. ABC

Word Power # 45: Feel Good or Feed Good

Each time I log on to Facebook I see some real wonderful posts. Many of them are quotes and powerful words to live by, stand by, survive by, and grow by. Many are really feel good quotes. They are feeling good because a large percentage of those who post them, really do not live by them or believe them. It feels good but it does not feed them. Do we want to feel good or be fed?

How many times do you have a conversation with your friends and you tell them what they want to hear so that they can feel good? Are these the conversations that they need or do they need to be given the truth so they can be fed? We agree with them because it makes them feel good. We give them our approval because it feels good. Why not give them more than a good feeling? Why not feed them with the truth?

Many people would be better today or more mature if they had people who would feed them well instead of allowing them to just feel good. I would rather you correct me and allow me to be better than, caress my carelessness.
If all we want is to feel good then we will constantly need to be propped up and cuddled. When we are fed well, we are nourished, strengthened, energized and prepared - ready for the journey ahead.

Dr. ABC

Word Power # 46: Because I am Happy

I made myself a promise to be happy – and I have been keeping it. Have I been sad? Do I have bad days? Do I know tears? You bet I do! But I am happy that I found out long ago that happiness is more of what is inside of me than what is outside. Someone's comment to me the other day was, "you seem to squeeze out and suck up every drop of enjoyment you can get out of life!"

Yes – he is right. I do. I purposely do and I honestly do. The fact of the matter is, my happiness is determined by me. My happiness was never connected to how many places I have been, the food I have eaten, the clothes I wear, the things I can afford, the things I can buy, the things I have done, my education or my car. My happiness was never connected to things – I grew up without lots of things and I made myself happy. I never had a birthday cake with my name on it until I was 25 but I was happy. I am the kind of person who makes use of all the opportunities offered to me.

You offer me steak and lobster and I am happy, I talk lots and I laugh out loud and I remember to tell you thanks for the dinner.

You offer me a KFC deal meal and I am happy, I talk lots and I laugh out loud and I remember to tell you thanks for the food.

I go on a trip to a far place or a fabulous hotel and I am happy, I talk lots and I laugh out loud and I remember to give thanks for the blessings I am able to enjoy.

I stay home and cannot afford to travel, I talk lots and I laugh out loud and I remember to give thanks that the house I am in is clean, safe and my rent is paid and for me those are blessings.

When I am dating or in a relationship, I am happy that I am afforded the company and connection of another.

When I am single I am happy to be alive, well, dateable and desirable.

Too many of us link our happiness to things. Here is my recipe:

Enjoy the moments you have
Enjoy the people you are with or only be with the people you enjoy
Be thankful and grateful for everything – people who deliberately count their blessings are happier
Ensure you foster happiness in your life today.

Dr. ABC

Word Power #47: Make Your Arms Long Enough To Do a Full Wrap Around

Has someone ever given you a real great big hug? I mean the hugs that are a full wrap around, where in that single moment you know you are secure, loved and appreciated. This full wrap around hug tells you that they gave you their best. It was not half-baked, half-hearted or half-done – it was a full wrap around. There is such a value in knowing that you have people in your life who will give you a full wrap around hug when you need it. But what happens when there is no one to provide that full wrap hug? What happens when you are alone? What happens when you need a push, a hand-up, a starter – what happens when your fuel is running on low? In these times you will need to wrap yourself. There is value in knowing how to comfort yourself, encourage yourself and speak life into yourself. There is value in making your arms long enough to give yourself a full wrap-around. One of my favorite songs is "Encourage Yourself" by Donald Lawrence & the Tri-City Singers, that keeps me grounded:

"Sometimes you have to encourage yourself
Sometimes you have to speak victory during the test
And no matter how you feel
Speak the word and you will be healed
Speak over yourself, encourage yourself in the Lord
Sometimes you have to speak the word over yourself
The pressure is all around but God is present help
The enemy created walls but remember giants, they do fall
Speak over yourself, encourage yourself in the Lord."

It is ok to look to others for a word of cheer and comfort
It is ok to look to others for emotional strength
It is ok to look to others for that push
It is ok to look to others for motivation
It is equally important to look to the inner you and pull out what is there. There is actually far more in you than you know.

Dr. ABC

Word Power # 48: You Don't Have To Use Words

A Russian lady moved in the house next door to me. Each morning I jogged by I would see her sitting on her front porch, cigarette in one hand, coffee (or so I assume) in the other hand. The first morning I noticed her I nodded and gave a smile and she nodded back. The second morning I did the same and she returned the nod and smile. This continued for months and the nods turned into healthy hand waves and the smiles got really big, almost to a grin.

We never said a word to each other and I don't know her name. What we had was a real healthy wave and smile between us. If she was not there on my jog back I would miss her and I think she felt the same.

A few months ago I stopped seeing her. I missed her. I wondered if she was ok.
Was she still physically able to wave and smile?
Was she still smiling?
Was she in a place where she could still smile?
Did someone do something to her and stop her from smiling?
Many thoughts went through my mind. After a few months of not seeing her I no longer looked out for her.

This morning as I was jogging I looked across a house in a different part of the neighborhood; I saw a hand waving to me and the biggest smile you ever saw!
It was my Russian morning smile – she was ok. I was happy to see her and, from the look of things, she was happy to see me. Nothing was wrong with her – she had her smile.

As I jogged home (or walked fast) I thought to myself about the impact she has had on me and the level of communication we had shared. We did not use words – we used our smiles and universal gestures to communicate. I am sure the smiles have many meanings and I feel like we had a real good relationship and strong communication through our smiles.

How do you communicate to others?
How do they see you?
Do you know if the people you smile at know what your smile means?
Do the people you smile at look forward to your smile?
Do not forget that you can show people the real you – you do not always need words. Try a smile – a real genuine smile.

Dr. ABC

Word Power # 49: Building a Bridge Only Makes Sense When You Need to Cross

I have been having some very serious conversations with myself lately about relationships and where I stand. I spent more than 8 years of my life dating 5 different people – all long distance. If you have ever engaged in a real long distance relationship, you will understand the effort that is needed and the bridge building that is necessary.

The other night I was walking home from a date and I thought about the effort that goes into building such a structure to allow people to get from one side to the other. I also examined the peril faced by those people of old who had to always negotiate crossing terrible waters, facing the possibility of drowning or being eaten by crocodiles all to get to the other side.

If you never needed to get to the other side then you may not have appreciation for the need for a bridge

If you have never needed to cross over something dangerous in your life then you may not have an appreciation for a bridge

If you have never needed to get to someone else on the other side then you may never understand the value of a bridge

In my walk that night I took a step back and thought about what it is that I really want. You may disagree with me on this one, but I know I have wasted some time trying to build bridges that I would not be able to cross. I had to take a step out of myself and tell myself I am not into building a bridge if I have no intention to cross it.

What bridge are you building?
Is a bridge always the right structure to invest in?
Can you get across the other side without this bridge?
Is that bridge necessary?

Should you leave bridge building to others and take the long way around?

Is the bridge you're building just a means of escape from the realities or should you actually be getting in the water to face your challenges?

Is that bridge you're planning on building just a fancy structure or is it actually needed to get you across?

Maybe together we will find the answers to these questions.

Dr. ABC

Word Power # 50: What's Your Number? Mine is 21.

I have always said that the teacher is still the single most important ingredient in the teaching-learning process. No matter how much technology is introduced, no matter how many tablets and iPads are in schools, smart boards, websites, learning videos, learning games, and apps, nothing can compare to a teacher who gives his/her best to each and every child. Every child, every teen, every adult student needs a teacher!

No matter how many school years I have had...it gets me every time I am done with a school year! This past school year I had the opportunity to impact 21 lives - I had 21 little people in my care. I had many more adults in college and university, but the 21 little people became my main focus each day.

I had 21 lives I could destroy with hate and bitterness or give them power to bloom and grow.

I had 21 lives that I could choose to inspire and ignite or ignore and ill-treat.

I had 21 children whose parents trusted me with their care, growth and protection.

I had 21 lives that I could remind each day that they are special, wonderful, and fabulous and could be exactly what they want to be.

I had 21 opportunities to be a big brother, a father, a friend, a confidant, an advocate, and a defender.

Here are bits and pieces of two notes I got a few weeks ago from parents:

What position of influence do you sit in?

Who has trusted you with their lives and development?

What role do you play in the growth and care of others?

What would you rather do than teach?

I do not take this vocation lightly - no teacher or leader should. I got 21 chances last year to change a life - how many chances do you have this year?

Dr. ABC
(Dedicated to Janet Clarke, one of the best teachers I have known for the last 14 years.)

Word Power # 51: These Pom-Poms Are For You

At the tender age of 16, I entered the working world. I was the Principal's secretary at a local primary school. To this day, I am not sure why Mrs. Barbara Reid hired me; I questioned if I would hire a young 16 year old boy just out of high school to be my secretary for a school with over 1800 students!

She saw something in me that I did not even see in myself. Of course, I always had dreams and I always knew I was heading somewhere, but at age 16 how much do you really understand about yourself? She knew I had just entered the game of life and career development and she assumed the role of cheerleader.

I look back, today, at some of the errors and mistakes I made on the job and how she would find a way to compliment and motivate me. I now realize that I was not as good as I thought I was. What I had was real support and someone who, regardless of the circumstances, would cheer me on! She believed in me. She is not one bit surprised about my accomplishments today. She always knew I was destined for excellence! She was a real cheerleader. She had her pom-poms ready from the very first day she interviewed me.

Who in your life needs a cheerleader?
Do you own a set of pom-poms?
Are you ready to make a cheer and jump cartwheels for someone who needs motivation?
Are you willing to build that pyramid and show that person they can stand on top?

In most games, the resident cheerleaders take the field at half time.
Half time is when many players are tired
The scores can be very discouraging at half time
Players on your team can lose faith in your abilities at half time
Some people wish they could change teams at half time

Some people lose faith in a game or their favourite player and leave the stadium or arena at half time
No one wants to be on the losing end at half time
Someone out there may just need you at half time. Get out your pom-poms!

Dr. ABC
(Dedicated to Mrs. Barbara Reid, past principal of Waterford Primary School, Portmore, St. Catherine, Jamaica.)

Word Power # 52: Obligated to Say the Right Things

I have always been someone who speaks up and speaks out. I am also someone who makes jokes and enjoys a carefree conversation. In all of that, I am mindful of what I say. I am very much aware that there is so much power in words.
"Death and life and in the power of the tongue" (Proverbs 18:31)

I believe in that verse from the Bible with all my heart. We have to think carefully when we are in a position to give advice, encouragement, praise or rebuke. Our words matter and they matter to those who have asked for you to share your opinion, support, guidance and admonishment.
A right word can allow someone to make life changing decisions. A timely word can save someone from jumping off the edge of life.
A rightly placed praise can give someone the extra push he needs to complete the task that seemed impossible

Words give life
Words give power
Words give determination
Words change destiny
Words build people
Words heal emotional sickness and diseases

The next time someone asks you for your advice, opinion or point of view, remember the power you have in your tongue and say the right thing.

Dr. ABC

Word Power # 53: Pride, Passion & Precision

I have been asked to write many references such as letters of recommendation, character references, etc. When I get those phone calls, requesting my help, oftentimes, I have to go back to whomever I did the reference for and remind them to live up to what I said. I also remind them to do their best, because I just gave them an excellent reference.

I made sure what I said about them would give them that job! I made sure the potential employee knew they would be getting nothing less than a star employee. I take pride in offering that reference. I know that whatever I write or say will impact that person and I am careful with what I say – there is a high level of precision that goes into its production.

Not only am I passionate about references but I am also passionate about my cooking! I love to cook, not for myself, but for others. When I invite anyone to my table, I get into a mood of pride and passion. Everything must be the best.

I cook with *pride*, knowing that what I offer others is a representation of myself. I can use many short cuts in fixing a meal for myself, but when it is done for others, excellence is the order of the day.

I cook with *passion*, knowing that I am serving others. I am glad to say that *service to others above self* was something that I was taught by both my mother and grandmother. They both reminded me of the value of taking the lower seat at times.

I cook with *precision*, knowing that this is not just merely a meal, but a representation of who I am. I ensure that the right amount of salt is used for flavour and the exact amount of pepper for taste. Everything is measured and everything is carefully placed in the pot at the right time.

People will eat, smile with you and then leave. But never be fooled for one minute. They do observe how they were treated. They observed how you served them. When we do for others, we must do it with pride, passion and precision. None of us are perfect and I am sure far from it. We all get tempted at times to just do what we can, any way we can, and move on. When this happens, ask yourself, would I personally want this? Would I prefer to eat this? Would I benefit from this recommendation?

When you do for others, do it with passion, pride and precision.

Dr. ABC

Word Power # 54: Stop Having a Bad Day Unnecessarily

There are some people who have a bad day on purpose.
They wake up and they know today is going to be a bad day.
They tell themselves it will be a bad day.
Travelling with others for years, having dinners, parties and going out, I realize one thing - people can really encourage themselves to have a bad day.

You have to be able to let it go. Let go of your anger, frustrations, and disappointments. Let go and have a good day.

The lady at the store was rude - tell her your mind or report her to the manager. Do not let that mess up your whole day. Move on with your great day!

You go to dinner. It was not the best meal as you had anticipated. Leave and say goodbye. Stop by the nearest burger place. Get yourself a big meal and have a great day!

Someone posts something dreadful about you on Facebook or tells someone something horrifying, repugnant or uncharitable about you. Read it. Learn from it. Grow from it. Avoid those people and continue with having a great day!

Too many of us have been responsible for having our own bad days unnecessarily. Have a great day!

Dr. ABC

Word Power # 55: Did You Settle?

I was talking to someone just the other day about relationships. I saw him with someone I assumed was his partner, and I asked how things were going. He informed me that the relationship did not work out but he settled for a special arrangement. He sounded very positive and that he had everything under control. Initially, he painted a colourful picture showcasing his content with the special arrangement, and it was now his new normal.

After a deeper conversation he opened up to me that he wanted more in a relationship but had to settle. He felt he was never going to meet a partner who wanted the same things he did so he thought it best to settle for a special arrangement. What are you doing with your life that has become a special arrangement?

Did you settle and forget to be all that you can be?
Did you settle and give up on those big dreams?
Did you settle and accept less than you wanted for yourself?

I have seen jobs I wanted to apply for but refused since I have applied to so many and did not even get an interview. Those moments pushed me to think I needed to settle for something less than I desired. I have a job that pays well and I am happy to do what I do - but that is not my dream.

Do I now settle out of fear of trying?
Do I settle because of all the past disappointments?
Do I settle because I know it is hard for a black man to get to certain levels in a country like ours?
Do I settle and do just what others expect me to do and be?

Do I settle?
Do I settle?
Do I settle?

We settle because we fear we do not have it in us to go the distance

We settle because we fear what others will say if we seem to be too ambitious

We settle because we fear what others will think of us

We settle because others told us NO - we can't go further, we can't get more

We settle because we fear this door may close soon

We settle because we are getting older and we don't wish to be alone

We settle because we fear if we ask for more we will lose those we have

We settle because we start to believe the narrative in our minds that we are less than, and we don't deserve more

I have no issue with someone who settles - just ensure that what you settled for is exactly what you want. If not, then your smile and confession of happiness will all be a farce.

Dr. ABC

Word Power # 56: Shine Now

Each time I meet people who share with me that the job they have now is just something they are doing until their dream job comes along, I wonder if they consider that their attitude on that job impacts their ability to find that dream job. Nothing is wrong with that premise, however, what concerns me is that many seem to be waiting for the dream job to shine. Many of us save our shine for that big break - a dream job, a special occasion, that special person.

Here is one of the issues I have with our churches today - we shine when we are in church and there is a big conference, visiting minister, pastoral anniversary, but we do just enough or less than enough when we are dealing with sinners - oh how we missed the mark! I remember being choir director back home years ago - my promise to the Lord was that I would direct that choir with everything in me every time. I did just that. I directed the choir with all that was in me whether it was church anniversary, Sunday night service, open air meeting, visiting some big church choir concert, singing at a national conference or some small church in the back of an inner-city community.

I used to be the leader of the church dance ministry in the Bahamas. They are a wonderful group of young ladies who impacted my life forever. After many years of ministry, we had impressive dances, won a few awards at the National Dance festivals and were highly respected among dancers. We received invitations to other churches to dance, and I can remember once we were going to a certain church in the ghetto (inner-city) area of Nassau. After selecting one of the best dances from our repertoire and the fabulous purple and pink costume, I was advised by a dancer that the church was very small, not many people would be there and the floor was made of very bad wood. She even advised that we all don't drive our cars to this rough area in fear they may steal them. I told her - that was the very reason why I chose this song and this elaborate costume. I wanted those people who needed it more, who did not expect Golden Gates Dance Ministry to come to their church, who did not expect a full troupe to turn up, and who did not expect us to offer them an award winning performance piece, to be given the best. I wanted them to get exactly what we promised God we would do for those who needed a light - shine! I remember that night the look on the little girls' faces who had never seen costumes and make -up so beautiful. They were inspired. They were motivated. They too wanted to dance. You do not get to choose when to shine. Once you get into that mode then you will lose it. You never know who needs your shine and who is watching.

A few weeks ago I went to speak to a group of 86 teachers - I put all I had into it - my shine
A day later a friend called me and needed some advice - I put all I had into it - my shine
When I am with my little kids at school in a classroom full of privileged kids - I put all I have into it - my shine
When I am teaching a room filled with immigrant black kids - I put all I have into it - my shine
When I'm teaching in an unfavourable environment - I put all I have into it even though I may be miserable at times - my shine

We do not get to choose when to shine. The next time you are tempted to hold back your shine, remember to always do your best or better because your mediocre efforts will reflect poorly on you and carry forward in your thoughts and attitudes in almost everything else you do. Do not give yourself the option of when to shine. I do not choose when to shine.

Dr. ABC
(Dedicated to all the dancers of Golden Gates Dance Ministry - Nassau Bahamas and the Choirs of Power of Faith Ministries in Portmore, Jamaica- thanks for the many years I was allowed to shine.)

Word Power # 57: Passion is the Secret

What makes us get up every day and be excited about going to work?
What makes us work full time, go to school part time, spend hours in the library and on the computer doing our studies?
What makes us follow our dreams and ensure we do what is required plus going that extra mile?

The secret is passion. Some people have no passion for anything. Nothing moves them, nothing excites them. Nothing propels and compels them. Have you lost your passion for life?

Why have you lost it?
Where did you lose it?
Who was there when you lost it?
Do you remember the place?
Can you identify the spot?

Let us go back and search for it. Let us find it. Let us launch a full out search for it. Let us cover the perimeter of our life until we locate it. Let us be honest and report it "missing", it's been well over 48 hours. It is now officially missing. Let us find it.

Without that passion, you will deny yourself excellence and success.
Passion, like any other seed, must be watered and must be nurtured.

Dr. ABC

Word Power # 58: Woe is Me!

A lot of us have an attitude of entitlement. We walk around thinking the world is always out to get us and everything and everyone is against us; the system, the school, the boss, and even the man who drives the bus. You think that your parents did not give you the best they could, and they owe you more. Instead, we should be far more grateful. Be grateful that they never aborted you. Be grateful that you were fed. What your parents owe you then really is nothing!

Now what did you do with the opportunities that were afforded to you like all of us? What did you do with your talents? Did you trade upon them? Did you bury them? As a matter of fact, have you even taken the time to discover what your talents are, or are you too busy complaining that you don't have the talents that the other boys and girls have?

Yes, this is a very strong conversation, but it is a necessary one. I would rather you be honest than nice. Honesty helps in our growth, nice will only allow us to feel better about our situation. I too know what it is to cry and feel sorry for myself. I think in the last 2 weeks I have also done some of this. What we want is solutions for our growth and development. We have to be all we can be and this attitude can keep us back.

Stop being the victim and decide to be victorious. Victory takes work and effort. A common saying is, success is 1% inspiration and 99% perspiration. Work seems like a curse word to many people today. Who wants to work hard? Who wants to work from 9 - 5p.m. and only get a salary? Who is willing to start from the bottom to get to the top? Stop being the victim. Decide to work and work hard. Give it all you've got. Use up all of you and work with what you have.

Dr. ABC

Word Power # 59: Be Kind to Yourself

Lately I have had to make some serious decisions. There is so much I want to do, so much I am being asked to do and so much others would love for me to do. There are also my dreams, aspirations, projects, ambitious ideas, 10 year plan, 5 year plan, and 2 year plan. There are people who need my attention and there are people I want to get their attention. There are things I want that are in my reach and there are things I desire that seem to be out of my reach.

This morning I entered the computer room with my kids. I was excited to continue to teach them more "magic" with our story writing series. We began to log on with much anticipation. We could not log into our computers. The Internet was working, but our usual password was not!

I called for tech support and they gave the usual direction but it did not help. I decided to no longer frustrate myself and the students and we started to have a family talk. I was upset since my lesson was not going as planned! My whole day was about to turn into a mess! Then suddenly a voice came to me - "Be kind to yourself."

There was nothing I could do to prevent this, so I had to just relax. My mind went back to all the things that were on my mind and I grabbed the opportunity to whisper to myself - "Be kind to yourself"

With all the fabulous technology we have - sometimes it just doesn't work out like we plan. What about us?

The next time you are at a place where you want to be hard on yourself - take a moment and reflect and maybe it is time to be kind to yourself. If not, you may just drive yourself crazy.

Dr. ABC

Word Power # 60: Perfect Days

I thank God that I have had many perfect days in my life. They may be many but I can track and count each one because of the PEOPLE in those days. Today, I watched a wonderful person get married and that was perfect. Congrats K Giselle Hunt. I sat with Lorraine Simms and Geraldine Romer and listened to Nicolette Archer who was the fabulous Mistress of Ceremonies.

That, in my book, is a perfect day!!!!! I came to the Bahamas in 2000 and left in 2008 and during that time I have called these ladies friends. I have been away 6 years, we have stayed connected and today, I was able to be in the same room with them. I was able to be the same 'ole' loud mouth, loud laugh, excited for everything, crazy Campbell they have come to appreciate........and for me that was a perfect day..... I wish for you all perfect days.

People make perfect day!

Not trips or money or gifts or clothes

People make perfect days!

Dr. ABC
(Dedicated to a wonderful friend Mrs. K. Hunt-Wilson for offering me another perfect day.)

Word Power # 61: The People We Tend To Forget

Like many other teachers, I have enjoyed watching the stars in my class shine. I have had students that I knew, from the day I walked into the class, that they would all become university graduates. In 2002, at St. John's College, I had a grade 5 class like that. They were all energized, motivated and keen to learn. They loved school. They loved that I pushed them hard and their parents loved my level of professionalism. Today most, if not all of them, are in universities all over the world as global citizens.

However, these were not my best teaching years. My best years were with students, whom I was not sure what would happen to them. They did not have the motivation needed for school. Many lacked parental support and involvement, and each time I pushed them, they felt threatened or attacked. These were the students I knew I had to teach, and these were the students that made me know teaching was my gift.

Back in 1995 at Waterford Primary School, I had a group of students like that. They knew they were not as bright as the others. They knew...they knew... but they did not know they would be better. That was where I started my teaching – I started by letting them know that they could do better. No matter what they heard before, no matter how many times their mothers came to the office, no matter how many times they were teased by other children, no matter how many books they could not read, they could do better. They believed me!

Children know when you are honest about helping them, and they know when you are saying nice polite words just because it is the start of the school year. These are what we teachers all say when we begin the school year. Yes, they believed me, but they held back their trust. They watched to see if I was the 'real deal' or just another teacher who would babysit them until June and be happy to pass them and their problems to the next teacher.

Here are a few tips. In whatever you do, take the time to focus on the people that need you most. They may not be the ones that shine but they are the ones that make you feel satisfied, fulfilled and accomplished at the end of your day. Get to know those people. Engage those people. Take them from where they are to where they need to be. Motivate and inspire. For these bundles of potentiality, it is more about laying a strong foundation of self-worth and having someone believe in them.

Dr. ABC

Word Power # 62: Come on Over – We are Having a Pity Party

The phone rang and I rushed to get it before it went to voice mail.
I was happy I got it - on the other end of the line I was getting an invitation - an invitation to a pity party.

This person was about to have a real throw down. Something bad had happened - their world had come to an end and I was invited to the party. I have been to a number of pity parties in the past.

I attended one last year, where someone lost a job and was about to jump off the building!

I attended a fabulous one, years ago, when someone caught a lover with another person and he was ready to take the lover's life and his own!

I attended another really fabulous exclusive one, where someone told a friend I know that he was not going to amount to anything. He decided it was time to give up on his dreams and passions since this one person gave him the advice that only one person can give!

A pity party is the last event you should allow anyone to force you to plan. Stand strong - stand firm - stand still and refuse any such invitation.

Are you having a pity party? Please do me a favour - do not invite me.

Dr. ABC

Word Power # 63: All is Well

Growing up in church and hearing the saints testify, you would always bet on hearing someone say "It is well." I was always concerned - as I knew things were not going well or as well as many of these people would testify. Were they lying? Should they have just told the whole church how bad things were? As I grew older, I realized that what many of them were doing was speaking life!

They were not lying.
They were not trying to prove anything to the neighbour.
They were not fake.
They were speaking life!

It drains your energy when you mope and mourn and complain constantly.
It drains your efforts when all you can foresee in the future is darkness and disappointment.
It drains your emotions when you cannot feel safe and secure in your next step.

Those old saints knew a secret that got them through those rough days - they spoke life!
Those old saints knew that telling every person they met on the street would not fix it - they spoke life!
Those old saints knew that better days were coming; this too shall pass, so they spoke life! One of my favorite songs back then carried these words:

When peace, like a river, attendeth my way,
When sorrows like sea billows roll;
Whatever my lot, Thou hast taught me to say,
It is well, it is well with my soul. (Horatio G. Spafford - 1873)

I can clearly remember two very rough times in my life when I grabbed hold of this song and made it my anthem! Today, it is well. Am I trouble free? Absolutely not! But I cannot allow my

efforts, emotions, and energy to be drained fearing my every next step.
Next time you are facing challenges - speak life!
It won't go away - but speak life!
You may need to cry - but speak life!

Dr. ABC

Word Power # 64: What Did I Get Myself Into

Many of you decided to go back to school this year. You were excited and some, a bit nervous. You have your dreams. You have your plans. You know what you want to be and now you decided to get there. You figured out how to pay for this school, since of course education is an investment and should be treated as such. You got the books, bought new clothes and now you are ready to get this party started!

The pressure is now on. There are expectations and accountability. There are deadlines and due dates. There are presentations and preparations. And let us not forget those dreaded group projects. It is a lot to do. You are reminded that success will take work and effort. Two weeks into the class you think to yourself - shit! What did I get myself into?

You are nervous as hell. This is the first time you've been back to school for a long time. You do not fit in since so many people at school seem younger. You are ready to stop - throw in the towel. This was a big mistake.

Was it a mistake?
Was deciding to follow your dream a mistake?
Was desiring more for yourself a mistake?

So as you ask yourself "What did I get Myself into?"
I will be the first to answer you by saying "You got yourself into the right spot!"

Dr. ABC

Word Power # 65: You Are Not Always In Trouble

A few months ago I went to Alberta. While waiting to board my flight, I heard my name over the announcement to see the agent at the gate. I went to the gate agent and she asked for my boarding pass. Of course I was thinking of all the people in this place they had to call the one black man in the area.
What did I do now?
Which killer had my name?
Who was on the no fly list that fit my description?
The lady said to me "I am offering you a free upgrade. You are such a pleasant gentleman. From the moment you walked to the check-in counter you were so polite and pleasant. You made my morning. Your mama must be proud of you."

When I was younger, I always thought that once I entered a room and people were staring at me they were saying something negative. When you grow up with lots of negative comments you get use to the possibility of the next comment being a negative one. When you live in a place where many people do not get to know how to always speak life, it can make you trust the words of a stranger less.
It can do that to you. That is why we need to speak LIFE to our children and those around us. I remember, back in Jamaica, one of my best friends pulled me aside when he saw my reaction on entering a restaurant. He said to me they could be saying a million positive things. They could just be saying:
"I like his height "
"I like his smile "
"I like the sound of his strong laughter"
"His skin is so black and beautiful "
Next time you hear someone talking about you, just remember, you are not always in trouble. Do not give into negative energy. Think life - Speak life - Give life!

Dr. ABC
(Dedicated to a dear friend Dunstan, thanks for reminding me that I am not always in trouble.)

Word power # 66: Sand in Your Eyes

I have been teaching kids for years. I have watched kids play in sandboxes for as long as I can remember. Oftentimes they would come crying to me. Why? Someone threw sand in their eyes or hair or on their clothes.

I try to tell them that this is possible when you are playing in a sandbox. Of course, before I can finish my sentence, they are back in the same sandbox with the same child playing again - another opportunity to have sand thrown in their eyes.

The only way someone can throw sand in your eyes is if you are playing in the same sandbox. Don't you know the sandbox rules? Too often you have sand in your eyes. It is full time we stop making the same mistakes and keep going back to play in the same sandbox with the same people. The next time you allow them to throw sand in your eyes – you may have a total vision loss.

Dr. ABC

Word Power # 67: Offer Your Pillow

I left for the great USA in August 2001 to go after my dreams. All my big dreams and plans were all wrapped up in this big trip to the USA to teach! It was not to be! My dream trip did not work out as planned. I returned to the Bahamas in less than two months. I returned to the Bahamas broken, hurt, disappointed, rejected, lost, and dejected.

I could hear the whispers of those who knew I had "failed" and those who thought I would have failed. I could see the faint smiles of those who were happy I failed. I would hear the gossip of those who thought they knew why I failed. I allowed none of that to move me – I closed my doors, went to bed and DREAMED AGAIN! I will tell you more about that next week.

I went back to the Bahamas, two weeks into the new school year. There I met Mrs. Romer, the Senior Mistress. I met her the first day I came to St. John's College. Within the first week, she gave me a ride home, invited me to her home and allowed me to sleep in her guest bed. To the onlooker, it may seem like the unusual and improper thing to do for a perfect stranger, but Romer was like that. She would help you no matter what. I don't think she knew what she did that day, but I needed that. She offered me her bed and her pillow. She handed me the remote control (that was the only thing I had control over at that time in my life). She gave me a Coke (that is the only thing she drank. I can't remember ever seeing her drinking water). She then closed the door. I lay in that bed and I just cried. I guess I just needed somewhere that felt more like home and the pillow that belongs to a mother – any mother.

I cried for all the things that I dreamt about that I thought would no longer be.
I cried for all the passion that I thought I lost.
I cried for all the things that were said about a little black boy from the islands that most of these American teachers I met in Atlanta knew nothing about.

I cried for all the disappointments I thought would now follow. I cried because I had to start over.

Jesus knows how to place someone in your life at the moment you need that kind of person most. I had just come back from Atlanta and I needed to cry, cry it all out as a cleansing of the experiences and lessons I learned from my time teaching in Atlanta – a real catharsis. It was a dark experience for me and it took away much from me.

Sometimes when you meet someone who is going through a rough time, you do not need to ask them anything – just offer your pillow.

Dr. ABC
(Dedicated to Geraldine Romer, a mother to many and a woman who has given so many strangers and passers-by her pillow.)

Word Power#68: Daddy Said I am a Star

I tell people all the time that growing up I was called many names by kids and others. Oftentimes these names were hurtful and deliberately set out to cause me pain and punishment.
But my father had his own name for me – he said to me always, "YOU ARE A STAR."

Someone called me sissy – daddy said I am a star.
Someone called me silly - daddy said I am a star.
Someone called me ugly and poor – daddy said I am a star.
Someone called me "battyman" – daddy said I am a star.
Someone said I did not have nice clothes – daddy said I am a star.
Someone said I was always wearing my brother's clothes – daddy said I am a star.

He pumped so much positive energy in me it never left me!!

I knew I was a star
I knew I was a boss
I knew I was handsome
I knew I was bright and intelligent
I knew I was a winner
I knew I was going to be great
I knew I was going to get a Ph.D.
I knew I was special
I knew I would graduate I KNEW BECAUSE MY DADDY TOLD ME SO – He said I was a STAR!

My father could not afford to give lots of things and send me many places BUT he gave me what was priceless and I still own it today – SELF ESTEEM & SELF – CONFIDENCE.
Be sure to speak life into your children and those around you.
Your single voice can drown out the many negatives voices.

Dr. ABC
(R.I.P Daddy October 31st would have been his birthday. Happy Birthday Daddy – you did tell the truth ---- I AM A STAR!)

Word Power # 69: Make Sure You Have People

A few weeks ago I was planning for my birthday party.
I was thinking about what to wear, my cake, the music, but
most importantly I was thinking about my guests. I was
especially thinking about my closest pals and the fact that most
of them would all be making the trip. This took
my anticipation and happiness to another level. These people
would have to pay the cost to travel and also some would need to
take time off from work. I stopped for a moment
and thought how deeply blessed I am to have people. There is a
special joy in knowing that the people you care about and think
about, care and think about you just as much!

I know what it is to be home alone, sick and have to make my
own tea, my own soup, force and talk myself into taking my
own medicine - we need people.
I know what it is to have the police find my next door neighbour
dead in his house (back in Atlanta in 2000) - he did not have
people - invest in people.
I know what it is to see others celebrate and no one to celebrate
with them - we must have people.

No PhD
No job
No fabulous clothes
No shopping trip
No special events
No vacations
None of these can compare to knowing that you have people.

I am not talking about the many people you have on Facebook,
Instagram, or other social media.
I am not talking about those who we say hello to now and then.
I am not talking about those who smile with you, but cannot
really stand the sight of you.
I am not talking about those who are only around for the good
times but lack the substance of true "peopleship."

I am not talking about those....
I am talking about the other people....

While you are investing in your 401K & your RRSP plans - plan
to invest in people.
While you are saving to buy that house - save the relationships
you have with people.
While you are investing in business and stocks and bonds -
invest in people.
While you are investing in your career and going for the degrees
- invest in people.
While you are building your personal empire – build people.
In all your getting - get people.

Dr. ABC
*(Dedicated to those special people in my life. The ones I know will
make me soup when I am sick, visit me in jail, lend me their coat,
listen to my stories, encourage me along the way, keep my secrets,
help me up when I fall, and ensure I look the best in my coffin when
I am dead.)*

Word Power # 70: Sometimes You Got to Build a Nest

I am not sure if, like me, your life gets so full at times; that you wished you had the power to fall asleep and wake up after all "this" is over. Well I just want to let you know that's a part of the package called life. I want to share a little trick that has always worked for me when I was having a real rough time and everything was seemingly going not as "planned".

Here goes. In the midst of all the confusion, trouble and worries, sit down and literally write down all the things you are thankful for. Every little blessing. Don't list the big obvious things that we are so focused on but list the things that keep us going and make us alive. Things such as:

1. The love of friends and family
2. Having a job
3. Good health
4. Having hands, feet, two eyes, hearing, and the ability to read this post all by yourself

A few years ago, while teaching in the Bahamas, there was a day when I was really down – down to my lowest. In a school of hundreds of students and teachers, I felt alone. Amidst all the noise and haste, a child noticed that a bird had made a nest right in the tree opposite my classroom. This bird made her nest less than 6 feet away from a room where over 75 students were dancing to very loud music and moving to the commands of a teacher with a very loud mouth. In the midst of all that, a bird found a place to make her home. That was one moment I will never forget. It made an impact on my life. The next time you come to such a place of turmoil in your life – stop and build a nest right where you are.

Build a nest and pray
Build a nest and love your enemies
Build a nest and do your best at whatever you do
Build a nest and be thankful

Build a nest and be a blessing to someone around you
Build a nest and protect your emotions and dreams and passions

Just because you're having a rough time or maybe going through some issues, you don't lose your value. You are still you and you will make it. Take this as an opportunity to build a nest.

Dr. ABC

Word Power # 71: The Lady with the Blue Belt

As a child, I grew up seeing my mother going to work every day as a nurse's aid (Registered Practical Nurse). When she took me to work with her, I was very excited. Being there I noticed three types of uniforms worn by the ladies on the nursing staff. The ones dressed like my mom wore a pink tunic over a white blouse, a hat with pink and white stripes and brown shoes. The second set wore full white uniform, white hat, and white shoes. Then, lastly, there was just one lady who also wore a full white uniform except her hat was made of lace, starched and stiff, like a crown and she wore a blue belt.

I asked my mom who she was.

Something about her was different and I liked seeing her with her blue belt. She was different and I did not know why. I was curious why she wore a blue belt. I intuitively figured out that she was important. When she came, people behaved differently. As a child, I did not understand the connections, but it fascinated me.

This lady with the blue belt was admired.
This lady with the blue belt had command of the room.
This lady with the blue belt had presence.

My mom told me she was the Matron; she was in charge of the hospital. Wow! I wondered why my mom did not want to wear a blue belt. Why did she not want her hat to be stiff and starched and made of lace? Did she think it was impossible to be the lady with the blue belt? Did she not want her blue belt also?

I was curious to know why. If things were different, would she go for that blue belt? Did someone prevent her from the blue belt? Did having us and taking such good care of us prevent her from getting the blue belt?

For whatever reason, she decided that the blue belt was not for her. My mom has lived a fulfilled, blessed, impactful life. She never needed that blue belt. It was never her plan or strategy. But how many of us refuse to go after our blue belts? Is there a blue belt you desire? Go after it now.

Desire more – desire a blue belt.

Dr. ABC

(Dedicated to my wonderful mother Doris Adina Campbell. You never wore the blue belt, but I know you were admired and respected for the over 25 years of service you gave to the Bustamante Hospital for Children)

Word Power # 72: It is no Chance – It is a Privilege!

"Thank you for giving her a chance."

These were the words a parent whispered to me today with tears running down her eyes as she was leaving our monthly Recognition Assembly. Her child was given an award for academic excellence. The previous night she sat in the audience of our annual winter concert and watched her little girl dance on the stage with all the other girls, full costumes, full make-up and all smiles.

Why was this special?
Why were the tears necessary?
Why did she need to say thanks?
Why the hug?

This winter, as usual, I did three dance numbers for the school concert. I had the usual star powers, the usual kids who shine, and the ones who love the stage and the lights and the costumes. I also had two children from our Deaf and Hard of Hearing Program, who wear cochlear implants. One of them, a little girl, who on the first day she came to dance class, I wondered what was I going to do with her. I had never had a child like this in my dance class before.

Would she be able to hear the music?
Would she be able to hear my loud voice?
Would she be scared of my shouts and "threats" when I needed excellence and would not accept anything less?

She was present at every rehearsal. I am not sure if she heard all the music or if she was just dependent on the counts or watching her peers. Whatever she did – she got it! She did not get it all 100%, but who cares, 100% is overrated many times!

Like all the other girls, sure enough, on concert night she was dressed up in costume, make up all done, and was on stage shaking her shimmy!

Today, her mom came to me with a gift, hugs and tears and thanked me for giving her child a chance.

Yes, I am the dance teacher
Yes, I decided on the costume
Yes, I decided on the music
Yes, I decided what flowers go in their hair
Yes, I decided the entrances and the exits
Yes, I decided on the moves
But, I am the one who is more privileged.

I was privileged to have that little girl trust me enough to want to be part of my dance club.
I was privileged enough to have that little girl believe I could see her like any other child.
I was privileged that her mom trusted me to allow her to shine.
I was privileged that I could have this job to touch another life.

I walked back to my classroom, humbled and blessed. We, who are in positions of trust, power and influence, must remember that we are responsible for the shine. It is OK to feel good that we helped someone to shine, but never forget the privilege you have to be trusted with that shine.

Dr. ABC

Word Power # 73: Don't Be Distracted by Those Who Are Absent

Have you ever been to an event and sat with someone who spent most of the time looking for someone else to arrive? Maybe you have been that person and have had that experience - I have. You are at an event and sitting at the table with that person. They spend so much time looking for someone who is not present. They keep looking at their watch, their phone, checking the time, looking at the door - just waiting for that someone to arrive. Nothing is wrong with waiting - the problem is, while waiting for that person to arrive, who sometimes never arrives, we miss out on what is happening around us.

Waiting for the other person to arrive, you miss out on the great conversations at the table by those who are present.

Waiting for the other person to arrive, you miss out on the smiles and the greetings from those who are present.

Waiting for the other person to arrive, you miss out on the jokes, laughs and joyful moments that are present.

Waiting for the other person to arrive, you miss out on the good food, hot soups, fancy drinks and other sweet treats that are present.

We spend all our present moments wondering about what is next. We spend all our effort waiting on the next thing to arrive. Stop and think about how many things present you have missed out on when you do this. The next event that happens in your life - enjoy what is present.

Dr. ABC

Word Power # 74: What Have You Changed Into?

As a child, l liked cartoons because the people in the cartoons could change.
I believed that when you had the ability to change that was a very special thing.
Bruce Banner changed into the Hulk when he was angry.
Peter Parker changed into Spiderman to fix the world.
Bruce Wayne changed into Batman to take revenge on criminals,
Princess Diana of Themyscira changed into Wonder Woman, used her lasso, bracelets and tiara to fight crime and evil.
The best for me was Thunder Cats, when Cheetara would change into the fastest animal I had ever seen, to fight crime and evil.

As an adult, I have come to value change and the impact of change on my own life.

I teach a course in change management for the University of the West Indies Open Campus and I am quite aware that many of us are challenged by the idea of change.

Change makes us uncomfortable
Change makes up scared
Change makes us nervous
Change makes us put up that wall
Change makes us become defensive

Change is, however, a good thing. When we change we grow, we evolve - we become. Of course, if I am going to be honest, I will also let you know that change can also be dangerous and painful and uncertain. Someone told me that she was separating from her husband, the other day. I asked why, you both seem so good together. Her response was "I do not like the person I change into when I am with him."

What impact do the people you engage with have on you?
Do they make you better after you have been in their company?
Do you change into a better person when you are with them?

Or do you change into a horrible person in their company, morphing into what they do and who they are?

When you leave their company, are you excited to be back or feel the need to take a shower?

Can you be you or must you change in order to be with them?

Ensure that as you change you are indeed growing. That change, like those comic book characters above, should bring you into a greater sense of usefulness and excellence - anything less is unacceptable.

Dr. ABC

Word Power # 75: Follow Your Heart and Your Passion

Far too many of us are waiting on others to co-sign our dreams.
Far too many of us are looking for others to give us the go-ahead
to dream.
Far too many of us do not yet realize that not everyone will
understand your dream or passion.
Far too many of us share our dream with dream killers.
Far too many of us wish we can have others to dream along with
us, so we wait and delay our dreams.

At age 16 I graduated high school. Most of my friends were going
to sixth form (which meant spending two more years in high
school at the advance level). I wanted to go to sixth form also. It
is what most people who were true academics did (or so
I thought). Most of the people I knew who went to sixth form
went on to medical school, became lawyers, PhDs, etc.

My mom told me I could not go. She could not afford it and, in
any case, my older brother and sister also did not go to sixth
form. They both went into the work force directly after high
school - so would I. At 16 years old and fresh out of high school,
it is very hard to get a job, a real good job. I applied to several job
postings.
I got a call from Air Jamaica, the proud national carrier at that
time. I was excited. I cannot describe the feeling. I was going to
be a flight attendant. I was going to see the world. I was going to
be young and fabulous in the sky.

The next call I got was delivered by a teacher who worked at the
local primary school in my community. The principal invited me
to an interview to be the school secretary. I could type, I was
organized and I loved to talk, so I would make a good secretary. I
was now happy to have, not one, but two interviews. I would
either become a flight attendant on the national carrier or a
school secretary at the local primary school. There was
no comparison! I was dreaming big! I wanted to see the world. I
was ready to be a flight attendant.

For the next week, an inner voice kept telling me to go to the school and choose that job. I was shocked. What a stupid inner voice! How could you tell a little boy with big dreams to not be a flight attendant? Planes take you places, I would meet millions of people, wear fabulous clothes every day and, who knows, I would even meet a rich movie star and fall in love! What was this stupid inner voice saying to me? How could a dusty school at the very end of my community, near the train tracks be the best place to invest my future or trust with my dreams? Yes, I did want to be a teacher, but come on, I was getting the offer to interview for a flight attendant!

Anyway, this voice did not leave me. I attended the interview at the local school, got the job, called the Air Jamaica office and informed them I no longer needed the interview since I now had a job. Somehow it felt good - it felt right and I knew deep down this was the right thing to do!

Well, a few hours later I told my dad and he gave it to me! "You must be damn X$%$X crazy! He was upset. How could I choose to be a teacher? What about being an accountant? What about being a doctor? What about being a lawyer? I knew he loved me and he wanted what he thought was best for me. I also knew that he did not understand my dream – it was not his to understand and that was fine with me.

I had a dream to be an educator and I needed to follow that with all my passion. Today that dream has led me to a good place and a proper space in my life. Not everyone will understand your dream – it is not theirs. Not everyone will cheer you on while going after your dream – it is not theirs. Follow your dream with passion and precision and it will lead you there – it is yours.

Dr. ABC

Word Power # 76: A World of Skittles and Saints?

Most of my posts on my Teachable Moments Facebook page have
been geared toward motivation, inspiration, edification and
my personal perspectives on many issues we all face.
It would be my desire to only talk about the good and uplifting
stuff. But sad to say, this is not how the real world operates.
Every now and then I am led to talk about some of the negative
things that we all face. Why? Am I giving it power and attention?
No. But if I refuse to talk about it and pretend that the world is
all skittles and rainbows and the people around us are
all saints and saviours, then I would be guilty of
being pretentious and that, of course, would go against
everything that I believe in and that is not reality.

Today I want to encourage us all to be aware of
our surroundings and the people we surround ourselves with.
We live in a world where some people do carry knives, spears
and daggers and will stick you when you are not looking
We live in a world where if some people think you are breathing
too much oxygen, they will attempt to destroy your lungs

They see you prosperous and they become poisonous
They see you progress and it becomes their problem
They see you reaching your destiny and they become dangerous
They see your desire and they become hazardous

When you wake up each morning, greet the day with a positive
attitude. Be motivating and inspiring and, in all of that, be aware
of the people you surround yourself with in life.

Dr. ABC

Word Power # 77: Show Me Where It Hurts

Growing up, I can clearly remember the many times I would play outside with my friends and I would get hurt.
I would fall from running too fast,
Get stung by a bee from climbing my neighbour's pomegranate tree,
Bust my head from playing in the gully,
Cut my knees from playing "stuck an pull" (tag),
Get dirt in my eyes from baking mud cakes for my neighbour's dolls,
Or hurt from being in a fight with some other child who I would be best friends with again, as soon as I stopped crying.

These were normal hurts for us as kids and we all knew who to show and how to get better – we would show our moms and they would fix it. They would use the famous and feared hydrogen peroxide, Band-Aids, warm towels, Vaseline, kerosene oil from the lamp or green bush rubbed together for the popular bee stings. There were also the times when we needed more, such as white cloth tied over our face for mumps or worm medicine for constantly scratching our butts. No matter what and how hard we cried, we would be ready to go back out within an hour! Mom had fixed it!

What I remember most were the times when I would run to my mom crying from some injury I got from playing cricket or some of the rougher games we played as little boys. There were no cuts or bruises to show my mom but I would be crying in pain. She would always say the same thing, "Show me where it hurts." As a child I knew my mom was a magician or like a real angel - she would be able to find out where I was hurting by asking me that one question! She had some real magical powers!

Less than a week ago, I was really hurt. Disappointed and heart broken, I needed someone to ask me where it hurt. This time it was different. I did not have a cut, a bump, a bruise or even a sore throat. It was on the inside. Funny enough, I was with my best friend who is also a medical doctor. He surely could have given me anything to make me better and of course he had the power to even write a prescription. Surprisingly, he allowed me to tell him where it hurt. For more than seven days, I told him where it hurt and he listened to me! All I needed was the love, care and concern of a friend. I have always talked about the power and impact of real friendship and again I proved my point. I knew, just like back in my childhood days, it was going to be OK.

Too many people suffer in silence because no one asks them where it hurts,
Too many people commit suicide because no one asks where it hurts,
Too many people make the same mistake over and over again, because no one is there to ask where it hurts.
Far too many of us are hurting and have no one to show where it hurts.
Invest in people – invest in caregivers. Invest so that when you fall and hurt yourself, there is someone who is concerned enough to say to you, "Show me where it hurts."

Dr. ABC

Word Power # 78: Don't Play Dead – It is OK to be Alive

A month ago in my class our topic was about Living Things. The children got into a real engaging discussion about what makes something living. They shared the text book responses that living things grow, breathe, reproduce, etc.
Soon after we had the "perfect" list, another child said that there were more things that living things do. They began to list other things:

Living things cry
Living things love
Living things can laugh
Living things can touch and hug
Living things dance and sing

Yes, they knew the textbook responses that we are so careful to include in our curriculum, but they knew more from being alive themselves. They knew that there were other attributes that made them consider themselves to be living.
Do you know you are living just because the textbook told you that you can breathe, eat, and reproduce? What makes you alive? It really made me wonder why, as humans and living things, we refuse to show that we are alive. We'd rather play dead.

Dead to our emotions
Dead to the hurts
Dead to the joys
Dead to the challenges

It is important that we be alive and stop playing dead
If you are alive then show those signs
It is OK to cry, laugh, love, touch, hug, sing, and dance
It is OK to be alive

Dr. ABC

Word Power # 79: The Right Age is Now

Just this week I was watching the popular competition show, American Idol. I was actually very entertained by the many young people who came with their big dreams in hopes of becoming a star. I could sense the passion, practice and promise in so many of them.

I was even more impressed as one of the judges was a past contestant, who is now a successful singer – evidence of what can happen when you truly follow your passion.

As I watched I kept thinking to myself

If I was 16 again, I would do this...

If I was 21, I would do that...

If I was 25, I would so do that...

If I was 30 again, I would so get into that...

I stopped myself in the middle of that thought and literally rebuked the very idea!

Why are you idly wishing what you would do if only you were 16, 21, 25 or 30 again?

What can you do now at 40?

What are you dreams at 40?

What are you going to do after 40?

What studies, hobbies, skill, or trade will you pursue at 40?

What will you invent, create, manifest, or challenge at 40?

What mountains do you plan to climb at 40?

What idea will you finally get the courage to pull out, dust off and set in motion at 40?

Stop getting carried away with the nostalgic concepts and what ifs...

Get to those things that you can do now and get to them today.

It would be sad if 10 years from now, I hear you say - if I was 40 I would...

Dr. ABC

Word Power # 80: Serious About More

8:30 Saturday morning.
It is -14 degrees outside.
I took a picture of people at the bus stop. I had to take this picture of adult learners heading to school. Most of these are mothers and fathers. They all came off the same bus. They did not drive to school in the comfort of their own cars. They are here on time to get what they need so that 2 years from now it will be better. They arrive in the cold and snow, this early, to put in the work so that it can be better.

As I sat in my car, I smiled. I was them just a year ago.
Up on a Saturday morning.
In the cold.
Trying to get more for my life.

Getting more will cost you
Getting more will take you out of your comfort zone
Getting more will take sacrifices
Getting more can be painful and challenging

When you see people enjoying their life with things and vacations and stuff and added pleasures-- just remember it takes work to get more!

Go get your MORE!!!

Dr. ABC

Word Power # 81: Caterpillar and Canker-worms

Four years ago an old college mate called me. He told me a really horrible story of distress and dread. He was having a rough time. He shared with me all the details (or so I thought) and I was moved to compassion. He then asked me to lend him some money. It was urgent and so I needed to act with the same urgency. I left my office and went to the bank, withdrew the cash and went to Western Union. The money was sent and I called him. He collected the cash within minutes and then about 10 minutes after deleted me from Facebook! I never heard from him again. This was no stranger - this was an old college mate. He took advantage of my trust and kindness – he stole from me.

Less than 2 years ago, someone else I knew asked if I could host them on their visit to Canada. He did not have anywhere else to stay and of course, knowing it was more blessed to give than to receive, I opened my doors and offered a pillow. This too ended sadly. He went into my room, searched through my personal and confidential belongings, and stole hundreds of dollars!

Today, as I was getting ready for work, it suddenly dawned on me that so much of what I have are gifts. I have pieces of clothes, things I use in my home, appliances, and so many more things. Even my Movado watch was a gift! It dawned on me that the money stolen from me could have been used to purchase so many of these things. But I never had to - they were gifts. God gave me back what the "canker-worm" stole from me. He gave me back what the "caterpillar" stole.

I cannot afford to become weary by dishonest people and forget the gift of giving. I will continue to offer a cup of tea, a helping hand, a pillow, a clean towel, a seat, or a glass of water. We must continue to give. After having way too many problems getting back money I lent to people, I swore I would not lend money again. I stopped me in my tracks and reminded me of the days when I never had money to lend.

Never allow anyone's dishonesty to make you become bitter or bent out of shape
Never allow anyone's malice to make you become manic
Never allow anyone's lies to make you listless
Never allow anyone's dishonesty make you fall into despair

Yes there are "Caterpillars" and "Canker-worms" out there, but there is also the "Farmer" who gives us newness each and every day!

Dr. ABC

Word Power # 82: Comfort, Peace, and Readiness in Trying Times

Today as I prepare to leave my home for my blessing (my job), I want to send comfort and peace and readiness to my many peeps who are not working and are consistently engaged in the job hunting process. Today I pray for nothing less than the same for you!

COMFORT until it happens.
PEACE to know it will happen.
READINESS for when it happens.

I reflect on my past and some of the most trying times I have had and the supplication I made for a change in my life – and it happened. I am aware that there are many of you who are going through stuff that you have become desperate and despondent wondering if things will ever change. Today I pray for nothing less than the same for you!

COMFORT to know that change will come.
PEACE to accept those things you cannot change.
READINESS to manage the change when it comes.

I know that the same One who gives seed to the sower, will do it in his time for you, and you, and you, and yes, YOU!

Dr. ABC

Word Power # 83: Must We Exhume the Body?

A few weeks ago I was dragged right to an emotional burial plot.
Of course, as I was walking to the grave site, I was upset and
it brought back so many feelings of loss, hurt and pain.

Someone wanted to exhume a dead body, so I was dragged
to the graveyard.

Nothing good can come out of an exhumation. No matter how
well you embalm that person, I personally think that having to
go back to the dead, the skeleton, the rot, is all just waste of your
time and energy – unproductive!

The next time someone pushes you to go to the graveyard - think
twice about it and ask yourself:

What good will this do?
What will you accomplish by digging up that which is dead?
What purpose will the dead serve you?

Leave which is dead – buried!

Dr. ABC

Word Power # 84: Exits and Entrances

It is a new year! How has it been?
Are you stuck in the same spot? Locked-up in the same areas of defeat and self-doubt? Have you gotten the courage to make an exit on those things and situations that have prevented you from fullness?

As we **exit** from the old one, there is an automatic **entrance** into another. That is how life is - there is no rest because for every **exit,** there is an automatic **entrance.** Don't focus on the fear, the hurt, the disappointments at the **exit**, but instead see the opportunity, the freshness, and the ability to start over at the **entrance**.

Take some time to balance yourself. Life throws so many things at you, it is your job to decide what to carry, what to pack, what to deal with. If you try to deal with it all at once - it will kill you!!! We must make some changes as we make the entrance – choose what to carry over with us. Remember we made an exit so that we could walk into newness.

Dr. ABC

Word Power # 85: A Little More like Sis Jackie

On February 7, 2015, about 6 p.m., I got a call that Sis Jackie had died. She was a church sister of mine and a real close pal when I attended Golden Gates Assembly in Nassau, Bahamas. For more than 7 years we danced together, ate, travelled, prayed, talked, laughed and encouraged each other. She travelled with me to Jamaica with the other dancers and was my second house guest when I moved to Toronto.

As I sat thinking about her and who she was, I smiled with satisfaction. A life well-lived. This was the perfect example of someone who you would not need to lie about at her funeral. This was someone that no one needed to embellish her life to make her look better at her funeral. This was someone who lived the life she danced about.

I tried to remember all the times I saw her upset or angry - maybe once?
I tried to remember all the times she cursed, shouted, or raised her voice - maybe once?
I tried to remember all the times she stomped out of dance class - never!
I tried to remember all the times she got so pissed that she decided not to dance the next day - never!
I tried to remember all the times I had to beg her to come and do what she promised she would have done - never!
I tried to remember all the many acts of kindness and words of encouragement - countless.
I tried to remember all the times she drove from her home to get me at my home when I never had a car - countless.
I tried to remember all the times I would hear her on the other end of my phone, "Bro Andrew, this Sis Jackie, hailing you up" – countless.

As Christians, one of our deepest desires is be more and more like Jesus. This morning, as I thanked God for her influence on my life, I thought how much better a person I could be, if I truly wanted to be a little more like Sis Jackie.

Dr. ABC (Still Bro. Andrew)
(Dedicated to Sis Jackie Allen, Nassau, Bahamas, 1957 – 2015.)

Word Power # 86: Being Resolute About Your Resolutions

It is now six weeks into the New Year. Did you make your New Year's resolution? Keeping it? One of my biggest concerns with the process is the number of people who within two weeks forget their resolution and resolve to go back to that which is easy, safe and familiar. Two words came to my mind as I reflected on the process - resolute and resolve. Far too often we are not resolute. We give up too easily and comfort ourselves by telling ourselves we will do it later in the year and possibly next year. One bad wind blows and we decide to throw in the towel and give up on the process and possibilities. When I examined the word resolute, there were other words that
were synonymous, such as purposeful, adamant and determined. There were actually a few words that gave me a lot of motivation, just by saying them. Words such as: determined, purposeful, adamant, unwavering, unfaltering, strong-willed and unshakable.
Oftentime, we fail to keep our resolutions because we have no resolve. We are weak and too easily distracted. As
a school teacher for years, I find that many students who fail are just way too easily distracted. They really want to learn, they really want their degrees, they really want that change, but they get distracted too easily.
They get distracted by the day to day hustle and bustle of being human.
They get distracted by the inner turbulence that we often face.
They get distracted by the plans and traps of those who do not wish them success.
They get distracted by the voices that say "you will never make it."
They get distracted by past failures.
They get distracted by their own inner negative voices of self-pity and self-infliction.
Whatever you decided as your resolution, stay focused, do not be distracted and ensure you remain resolute!

Dr. ABC

Word Power # 87: Winners Walk Away Too

When I was young and would get into a fight or confrontation, the worst thing I could do was walk away.
Walking away said you were weak, scared and could not stand up for yourself.
Walking away said you were a sissy and that invited others, even weaker than you were, to now have power over you.
Walking away also meant that those who wished to hurt or harm you now knew that you were weak and they would not stop coming after you.
If you walked away, you would never be given the title of "winner."

I grew up knowing not to walk away from those things that confronted me. That was actually a really good quality I got from my mother, and more so, from my grandmother – Sister May.

However, today, I know that the process of walking away is not always a sign of weakness or defeat.
Walking away can actually be a sign of real strength and determination.
Walking away can be seen as winning and successful.
Just a few days ago, I had to make a really strong decision to walk away.
I realized I was in a constant fight and losing.
Walking away made me a winner.
You do not need to fight every enemy or engage in every battle.
At times, you are an automatic winner if you just walk away.

Dr. ABC

Word Power # 88: You Must Forgive

Let no one hurt you or offend you so much that you can't let it go. Let it go and hold on to life's newness. Forgive as you have been forgiven. That feeling of refreshing you get afterwards is priceless! Forgive and apologize when you must and even those times when you don't think you should. Clean up and let go and breathe in all the newness of life! See how big you feel. You are a giant of a person.

People use us and hurt us and discard us. It eats away at your being to be involved in the mess it takes to plan a revenge or talk about them. Negative energy and thoughts eat you up and make you sleepless and restless.
You know you are right, but take the phone, make that call, write that letter of apology, say you are sorry and you forgive them for the things they did. Then put down the phone or the pen and give God thanks for all his mercies towards you and see how you feel afterwards.

I know the human part of us wants to see them pay or hurt or prove that we were right. God knows and you can't sow corn and reap peas. Harvest day will come and you will see. Love you and take care. I pray that the God himself that comes in my room here in Toronto and comforts me, will do the same for you!
You don't need to be friends or be in touch after that. Just clean up and move on! Don't worry about if they will laugh at you or call their silly friends to say you are weak or you lost the fight. Forget that. Nothing compares to the inner peace you get after. Seek peace and pursue it!

Dr. ABC

Word Power # 89: The Computer is Not Working

In my computer class at school, oftentimes, a child would tell me that their computer is not working. Nine out of ten times, they are really not doing the correct process. What I usually do is ask that child to shut down the computer and use another one.

I would then ask another child to go and use the same computer that was not working. That child would then log in, bring up his work and get the job done! The computer is working and now the first child would have to decide what he did wrong. We have proven the computer is working, now let us figure out what you did wrong.

It is very easy to blame others, the system, the environment, and everything else to feel good about our failures.
What about taking the time to figure out what we did wrong.
What was our contribution to the error?
What could we have done better?
What can we do differently?

The next time a computer in your life is not working - do not log off or shut it down. Stop and think - "What did I do wrong?" Just maybe, it is an easy fix if we take the time to analyze ourselves and attend to the errors.

Dr. ABC

Word Power #90: Keep a Close Eye on Me

We are so busy minding our own business that we forget
the power in helping others. We are also so busy trying to be
liked, we forget the power in honest and open dialogue
and correction. We are so careful with our words that we end up
saying nothing of value.

I know correction is hard but I would rather the critique of a
good friend who has my interest at heart any day, over an enemy
who smiles while they watch me go over a cliff. The other day, I
was very strong with a few of my university students. I was very
firm. I gave them the talk that you give to loved ones, people you
care about. I did say some strong things, but of course that was
my intention. Twenty four hours later I got the following email
from a student:

Hi sir,
You have really been an inspiration to me thus far. Whenever I am
overwhelmed and I hear your voice, it's as if I get the energy I need
to push even harder. I will admit sometimes I felt confused and
stressed out with my studies and life around me but I am so
determined to be successful in life that failure will never be an
option for me. Presently I am doing three continuous assessment
courses with great similarities and with all the activities and
graded assignments I don't even have time for anything else....I
believe in appreciating things because I know other people who
will do almost anything for this opportunity. My wish is you keep a
close eye on me and help me steer back on track if I ever lose focus,
not saying I will but no one knows what the future holds.

What if I had ignored her and allowed her to just do her thing
and fail? Keep your eyes on others you care about - a shepherd
watches over sheep - that is just what we do!

Dr. ABC

Word Power # 91: What is Your IP Address?

Recently, I went for a visit back home to Jamaica. I noticed my
Facebook pages feeds were all about Jamaicans. All the events,
updates, advertisements, and liked page suggestions
were Jamaica related. It dawned on me that my computer knew I
had changed places. The technology we now have has that
ability. My computer and phone switched the time automatically,
the moment I touched down in my native land. The technology,
GPS, and location abilities allowed social media to know where I
was.

So many people today have no idea where they are in life.
They do not know their IP address
They do not know who "feeds" them
They do not know who is "posting" in their life
They do not know who "likes" their situation
They are not sure who is "promoting" their life

They have logged out! They are disconnecting from their
tracking devices!
They have allowed situations to force them to disconnect.
They have allowed malicious people to push their disconnection.
They have allowed life challenges to loosen their connections.

We must be able to change with our IP address when
life automatically pushes us to change. Far too many of us are
lost because of major changes in our lives. Do not get left behind
in a place where you do not even know where you are.
Don't be so disconnected from your life, emotions and
current situations that you cannot locate yourself.
Like a Facebook page, keep current with the things in your life
that concern you, the things that impact you, the things that
shape you, and those that influence you.
Never lose contact with who you are, where you are, and where
you plan to be.

Dr. ABC

Word Power # 92: Take Care of Number One!

Last year, December 2014, I celebrated a birthday milestone. A friend called me a few weeks before and asked me why I was planning my own party.
I told him why not.
I wanted a party to celebrate my 40th birthday.
I wanted this to happen and I know I was the best person to make it happen.

Yes, it would be great to have someone take the reins and throw me the party of my dreams. But since there was no one, why sit and mope and wish and wait?
Why not take care of number one?

Way too many of us have given the responsibility of taking care of number one to someone else.
That is why we are so easily disappointed, easily hurt and easily heart broken.
I do believe there is someone out there who will take care of number one like I desire, but in the meantime, I must take care of number one myself.

I will continue to plan my own events and take care of number one until someone comes into my life that can do the planning.
I cannot afford to
Not live
Not be
Not have
Not do
Because I am waiting for someone to take care of number one.
Who knows, I may even plan my own funeral - and I will be fine with that too.

Dr. ABC

Word Power # 93: How Prepared are You for Your Blessing?

I like to hear people talk about their next big move.
The plans they have for their own development and if you know
me, you know, I believe in having dreams. My only concern with
a number of people is that they have no actual movement plan.
They talk of a blessing coming but they have made
no preparation. What I know of blessings (and this is from my
Sunday School days) is that there has to be something to start
with.

The 5000 people that were fed with a child's lunch - 5 loaves and
2 fishes.
The water that turned into wine began with vessels filled with
water.
The woman healed with the issue of blood pressed through a
crowd.
There was something to work with.
Many people want to be blessed but are not prepared to handle
it.

How prepared are you for your blessings?
You want to own a car - have you done any driving lessons?
You want a degree - have you researched any schools?
You want to ensure you look youthful and healthy - have you put
in the work to maintain yourself?
You want to fall in love and live happily ever after - have you
been preparing yourself to be a good partner?

Be careful that when your blessings finally come, you are
not prepared.

Dr. ABC

Word Power # 94: Distracted by Bitterness

Let no one offend you so much that you become bitter.

Bitterness will age you.

Bitterness will stress you.

Bitterness will deform your happiness and malfunction your dreams.

Let it go and move it. It is not easy, but it is possible.

Think love.

Think forgiveness.

Think mercy.

Do it not for them. Do it for you.

Work on you.

Fix you.

Care for you and never let bitterness distract you.

Dr. ABC

Word Power # 95: Earn Your Stripes

We live in a world where everyone wants to be in charge.
Everyone wants to lead and not just lead, but lead overnight!
One of the first things I learned, as I specialized in leadership,
was that a good leader is also a great follower.

Everybody wants to be the Boss
Everybody wants to be the Don
Everybody wants to be the Diva
Everybody wants to be the Legendary
Everybody wants to be Miss Thing
Everyone wants to be - the one - the only...

Words like Diva, Legendary, Principal, CEO, are reserved for
those who have proven...
Many people today do not wish to prove anything.
They walk out of college and they immediately want to be the
head cook!

Excellence takes work and evidence.
People respect you when you have proven your worth.
One of the first steps in growing is to know what you
know, admit what you do not know, and be interested in
knowing what you do not know.

Take the time to invest in knowing your craft and earning your
stripes.

Dr. ABC

Word Power # 96: You Are Not Just a Circle

Having a fabulous Math class with my students and we got into a discussion about the "CIRCLE" I had on the board. A few months ago the circle was a 2D SHAPE
A few weeks after that same circle was back again as part of a CONE,
later it was a CLOCK.
I took that same circle in the Science class and it was a part of a MACHINE
A few weeks ago that same circle was a PIE CHART
Last week that circle, in fractions, was a WHOLE
Be careful what you assume about someone, they may look like a circle, but are they really?
Get to know people for yourself and do not allow anyone to tell you who they are.
Allow no one to force you to be just a circle - there is so much more to you!

Dr. ABC

Word Power # 97: He Kept Me (Part 2)

The HOLY GHOST can choose some untimely place to have a praise break. I am sitting in Starbucks and this is the place he chooses to wrap his arms around me and remind me I am loved. JESUS! I love you. I can't make that loud vocal shout in this place. But I have to get it out here in writing.

New mercies I see each day. I could have been dead, in jail, a murder victim, out of my right mind, ready to jump, but he kept me. Not just to God but also to the best friends who helped in that keeping. I am thankful to them also. Whoever or whatever you give thanks to, make sure you give thanks.

I could have been dead, jumped off the library roof back in college. I could have been murdered by the guys who hated me for what they thought I was. I could have died of depression when I had no one in church I trusted enough to say how I was hurting. The times I owed so much school fee and had no idea how it was going to be paid. For all of this and more he kept me.

Kept me from jumping.
Kept me from stealing.
Kept from dropping out of school.
Kept me from those who planned my hurt.
Kept me from lies and malice.
Kept me from giving up.
Kept me from wicked neighbours.
Kept me from unloving church people.
Kept me from bad minded "friends".
Kept me from hurting myself.
Kept me from losing my mind.
KEPT ME. KEPT ME. KEPT ME. JESUS KEPT ME. I will not be afraid or ashamed to say HE KEPT ME.

Dr. ABC

Word Power # 98: Reciprocity and Balance

December 2014 I declared that the year 2015 would be the year of reciprocity and balance in all my relationships and interactions. I must experience measurable, tangible, and honest reciprocity. So happy I did that.

Talk about self-sorting!
Talk about the lines falling into place!
Talk about being able to see true colours!

I was so happy that I made that decision. People will always show you who they really are if you just allow them. There must be some kind of reciprocity and balance - anything less than that and someone is being used and abused. I examined all my interactions and tested the worth and value of a few. I will continue to welcome into my life as I move into 2015 and beyond, people who wish to share and reciprocate and add balance.

Have a bless day peeps. Make sure you have balance with everyone you interact with. Give more than you take. Give things with great value. Things like hugs, prayers, best wishes, kindness, good ethics, kind words, good advice. Share your talents , give motivation, give inspiration, lend a helping hand, honest responses, etc. And when you genuinely have nothing to give, that is ok - you have what you had.

Dr. ABC

Word Power # 99: Even a Bitch Knows When to sit still

To all my peeps who may be going through some rough time, I am sending you some positive vibes. I know the world gets messy at times and the load is too much to carry. I wanted to stop by to tell you:

Cry if you must
Rest if you must
Be alone for a while if you must
Vent if you must
Shout if you must
Pull away a bit if you must
Choose to be yourself for a while if you must
Walk away from it if you must

But never give up. Take it from me. There were times when as far as my eyes could see, was just disappointment, set-backs, hold-ups, drag-downs, buss-up, judgment, shame, weakness, what-ifs, what-now, what-next, when-will...

Figure out the resource you will use to keep sane
Figure out the resource you will use to keep awake
Figure out the resource you will use to keep you from jumping
Figure out the resource you will use to wait until and hold on still

Talk to a friend - ask for help if you need it
Talk to a stranger - strangers are good listeners
Listen to songs - songs can save lives
Pray - it works and gives inner peace
Sending you nothing but some real love and real talk.
Life can be a bitch!
But even a bitch knows when to sit still.

Dr. ABC

Word Power # 100: Where is Your Support System?

The other day I had an interview for a very important undertaking. They informed me that the process would be very intrusive and they would be digging into my past. This was intended for me to have a better understanding of who I was, who I am today and who I intend to be. One activity that left an indelible mark on me was when I was asked to list every member of my family and close friends and say what support, if any, I got from each person.

This was a real eye-opening activity for me. This woman had serious professional skills and the questions she asked would not allow me to escape my honest emotions. No stone was left unturned and she pushed me to a place of emotional responsibility and accountability. It was painful at times when I realized that I was not as supported by individuals as I thought I was or hoped to be. It was also comforting when I realized that, indeed, I had strong support from others.

For those instances where I knew I was not supported and continued to hang on, though at times I could see the breaking thread, I decided to let go. She reminded me that this was a healthy way to deal with loss and way too many of us refuse to deal with the loss so we hang on to broken, fragile threads. Many of us have in the past, in times of dire need, have reached out for support, only to find ourselves falling, because what we thought was a strong rope was only but a rotten, broken thread.

In a world where we will need the support of others, let us make sure we know where that support is.

Dr. ABC

Word Power # 101: Speak Your Own Truth

So there has been much debate on Facebook concerning Baltimore and, in extension, Black Lives in the USA, and issues of race, class, privilege, etc. It seems to me that many black people are unsure if they can engage in this discourse since they have many white friends, their boss is white and the many future opportunities they are looking towards are held and offered by white gatekeepers. I guess you can imagine their "predicament" Having many white friends does not disqualify you from speaking YOUR TRUTH. Your white friends will not be intimated by YOUR TRUTH. Since I moved to Canada, I have gained the pleasure of having many white people in my life (who knows, the great lover I have been waiting for may just be white) – people who are honest, genuine, accepting, loving, kind, and wonderful.

I can always be (and will always be) myself when I am with them. I don't need to "dress white" "act white" "eat white" (and you know me and food okkk). I can be just me and that is fine and I appreciate them for being them.

My mirror will never allow me to forget I am black.
My history established that I am black.
The many systems I have encountered as a professional in Canada remind me I am black.
The present practices and injustices will keep reminding me I am black.
The doors that I had to kick down confirm I am black.
The closed doors I had to walk away from signal I am black.

So do not think for one minute that because I have white friends I automatically lose my voice. I will never be intimated to talk about issues that impact my black body. My white friends and co-workers know who I am – they know I am black – trust me they do! They respect my voice. They may not always understand my fight- that is fine; it is my fight, not theirs. I will continue to fight my own battles, talk about the issues that impact me.

I consider myself to be an ADVOCATE LEADER, I am therefore CALLED to speak out and act on behalf of those who are downtrodden, vulnerable, excluded, and pushed-aside.

I am a leader.
I am a teacher.
I am a friend.
I am a son.
I am a Jamaican.
I am Canadian.
I am Black.
I ... am ... Black...

Dr. ABC

Word Power # 102: **Guard Rings**

Someone working hard to figure out my success and journey finally asked me if the two rings I wear most often are guard rings!!!

I really had a good laugh.

When you don't know the value of hard work, passion, consistency, late nights, early mornings, sacrifices, and then your belief is rested in TRICKERY!! I actually do have "guard rings" each with two big stones – PASSION and PERSPIRATION.
Tell people the truth about how you made it over!!
Tell them what keeps you sane in a troubled world like ours.
Tell them what keeps you centered in a place that so easily is imbalance
Tell the young people who want everything in sight how you worked for it. Unless we do, they will still believe there is an app for that!!!!!

Dr. ABC

Word Power # 103: I am Having a Bad Week

Just a week ago, I had one of my very good students in my class display some upsetting attitudes. He loves math and we had just finished a really exciting math class. Everyone was now ready to demonstrate their own learning by completing some written activities.

He sat there and was doing nothing. I passed by his desk and reminded him more than four times that the activities were time sensitive and I needed his book.

One hour passed ... nothing
Two hours passed... nothing
Kept him inside for recess...nothing
Decided to leave him for a while... nothing

I was actually very disappointed. He is a good student and I was not sure what was happening. I walked over to him and asked all the necessary questions we would ask at this point. He did not have much to say. I ended by letting him know that I was still very much proud of him, I loved him, I knew this was not his regular attitude, and that as soon as he was ready to work again I would be here. I went back to my desk.

Two minutes after that he came to my desk. "Sir"
I looked up and it was the same student.
"I am having a bad week."

Remember to tell those who may have been distracted or disappointed at times, that there is yet so much promise inside of them.

Dr. ABC
(Dedicated to all the students I taught during the last 20 years. I learn so much from teaching you.)

Word Power # 104: There is So Much More Inside of You

I teach online and so very often I have to print quite a bit of stuff. I have a new printer for my home office. This new printer is quite fancier than the one I had before. This one tells me, using a pop-up graphic, when the ink is low and gives me a basic idea of how much is left.

For the last two weeks, each and every day I print, the window warning message comes up and warns me that the ink is low. This morning, as I was about to print nine sheets of paper- sure enough the window warning message popped up - ink low!

I watched the printer as it pushed out 9 well-inked pages. There was way more ink in this printer than I imagined!

Sometimes we allow too many people to "pop up" with warning messages whenever we have a dream, idea or a new venture. When this happens we distrust ourselves, we lose confidence in our abilities, we question our paths, and we get timid about our ventures and lose the passion we started out with.

Yes, your ink may be low - but there is still so much more in you!

Dr. ABC

Word Power # 105: Hug Someone Else

If you know me then you will know I am a hugger.
I have hugged people in the past that did not expect a hug, others may not have wanted to be hugged, others did not think they deserved a hug and others did not know how to receive a hug.

Far too many of us has not been hugged and do not understand the meanings behind hugs.
Far too many of us have been so hurt we are scared of a hug.
Far too many of us only understand a hug from a sexual place.
We have far too many angry people walking around who just need a hug.

Hugs remind us that we are loved and cared for.
Hugs tell us that we can be safe.
How many times have you broken down just when you got a hug?
How many people do you know that are in need of a hug?

Previously, I encouraged us to make our arms long enough to hug ourselves. Today I exhort (yes I said exhort) you to make those arms even longer so that you can hug someone else.

Dr. ABC

Word Power # 106: Only a Fool Competes with Spectators

In every big sport event, there are two distinct set of people - participants and spectators. I have had occasions in my life when it is clear that people who are not even in the race are trying to compete and distract. I smile when this is clear to me and then I ask myself a few questions:

Why would you be distracted by spectators?
Why would you leave the track and try to compete with spectators?
Why get upset when spectators come onto the track?

Spectators are behind the fence for a reason.
Spectators spend their time cheering, eating snacks and having a good time - they are not in work mode.

Runners are on the track because they are either trying to qualify or have qualified.
Runners are on the track because they are dressed and ready for competition.

Stop wasting your time responding to, being distracted by, and competing with spectators!

If you are a true runner - focus your efforts on the track!

Dr. ABC

Word Power # 107: What Are Those Lines in Your Face Mama?

This past Mother's Day, I spent some time on Facebook just looking at all the pictures of mothers being posted. I took some time to think about all these Caribbean mothers and I examined the stories I could see in each picture. Most of your mothers, like mine, are in their 50s, 60s, 70s, 80s and even 90s. A great sense of pride, respect and admiration swept over me. I looked at the faces of many of these Caribbean women and the lines in the faces and I was so in love!

Those lines in their faces reminded me of the hard work, courage, stamina and persistence that they demonstrated. Many of us are blessed to have mothers who really worked to get us where we are today.

Mothers who farmed the ground in the hot Caribbean sun to ensure we had food to eat.

Mothers who made sure our clothes were clean and spotless and have never seen a washing machine in their days.

Mothers who would fan us and keep us cool through the hot Caribbean sun and had never used an air conditioning unit.

Mothers who worked hard, saved everything they had in order to pay school fees and buy books, as they saw education as our way out of poverty.

Mothers who did without so we could have.

Mothers who exposed us to things and opportunities that they themselves could only read about in books (if they could read).

Mothers who spent all night praying for our safety, when we were out all night dancing and carrying on.

Mothers who expressed their love for us in ways that
North America cannot understand and protected in ways that we
will never understand.

Love and respect to ALL mothers around the world,
your experiences may be different from that of many of
our Caribbean mothers, but your love and expression
of sacrifice is no less! I just wanted to tell my own story to add to
the history!

Dr. ABC
*(Dedicated to my mother, who did without so many times so that I
could have.)*

Word Power # 108: Leadership in Your Community

Today I want to speak to you about leadership in your community. Maybe you are wondering to yourself - leadership? I am not a leader. I am just about to graduate - what is he talking about. Well, you are all indeed leaders. You are leaders in your family and some of you are leaders in your community. Your community is not just where you live or sleep, but where you interact with others, be it at home, school, place of worship, work, or any other organization.

If you are responsible and accountable to anyone else other than yourself - then you are a leader
If your actions impact and influence those around you in any way - then you are a leader
If someone is looking to you for guidance, advice, motivation or inspiration – then you are a leader
If you have been given an opportunity to impact lives at any level, be it as a parent, caregiver, supervisor, or manager – then you are a leader.

A leader is a person who influences a group of people towards the achievement of a goal.

There is a call for inclusive leaders. There is a call for advocacy leaders.
There is a call for leaders who will think of others above themselves.
There is a call for leaders who will not ignore and turn a blind eye to the need and cry of those who are most vulnerable among us.

How do you ensure that the people around you feel included?
How do you navigate a place like Toronto, with its mix of many cultures and personalities?
How do we show authentic respect and appreciation for the diversity around us that makes this place special?
For too long we try to tolerate others.

Inclusive leadership is not about tolerating others.
It is about educating ourselves about what makes us different,
appreciating those differences, and moving to the place where
we can celebrate those differences.

Dr. ABC
*(Excerpt from graduation Speech made at Oxford College, Toronto,
June 3, 2015.)*

Word Power # 109: Sitting on Seeds

Most of us have figured out what others can do for us. We know what our parents can do for us, what our friends can do for us, what our employers can do for us, what the government can or should do for us, and what the "system" can do for us.

Now that you have figured out what others can do for you, let us now work on what you can do for you. This may be a rough statement when in your mind you are thinking "I just need help!" But stop and ask yourself, what can I do for me. It is indeed a harsh realization for some of us who have become so used to asking for everything and we live in a world where so many of us have been taught how to be helpless!

We do not want seeds – we want fruits.
We do not want seeds –we want instant results.
We do not want seeds – we want the bottled experience now.

Start thinking about the value of having seeds. What are you doing with your one seed? Are you planning to plant it, or is it easier to ask for a fruit? Why not plant it and then ask for water, manure, and extra sunlight instead. Nothing is wrong with asking for help. But ask for the help that will ensure your success. Far too many people are sitting on seeds and asking for fruits.

Dr. ABC

Word Power # 110: Customer Service

Dear Trinidad

As a black Caribbean national, when you go to other islands you are mentally prepared to be treated like a second class visitor. Well you took me by surprise in a very significant way. The kindness, respect, hospitality and smiles will last for a long time.
To the staff at the UWI Inn - 99%.
To the security - 99%
To the lady in the Chinese restaurant - 100%
To the conference people - 100%
To the taxi man who helped me buy a pair of reading glasses since I lost mine on the first day -100%
To the mango man- 99%
To the people in charge of food - 150% (I am the "teacha" so I can give "dat". So no "badda" start "fi" complain)
You are all on my honour roll. One love. I guess you all know the power and value of customer service. Funny thing is this was a conference on "Best Practices" and I guess everyone got the same memo.

Dr. ABC

Word Power # 111: Stay Home With Your Bad Mood

None of us is perfect. No matter how positive you are, we all have our bad mood days. What we forget is that a bad mood is as bad as a bad cough. Once you are out in public, people see and hear. You can hardly control yourself and you upset, offend or distract others.

There are some of us who like to go out in public with our bad moods. It gives us the attention we seem to be lacking. We get pity and some will even throw us a pity party. Other times, unknowingly, we give the virus to others.

People ask me if I ever get depressed or down. They ask me if I am ever sad or unhappy.

What?

Of course!

The reason why you don't get to see me sad and depressed and unhappy is because at those moments I take a time out. I choose not to be in a crowd and spread my virus. When I take that time to reflect, cry, and be alone, my spirit is restored and I get to deal with my emotions and put life into perspective.

The next time you are in a bad mood, stay away from the crowd and deal with your emotions. You will see the energy that you have and the light that shines from you when you re-enter the crowd.

Dr. ABC

Word Power # 113: I am Grown

One of my favourite songs now is from the legendary Beyoncé, "Grown Woman." The chorus is a powerful line, "I'm a grown woman, I can do whatever I want."

A lot of us love that song, because it gives us permission to be whatever we want without seeking consultation or advice from anyone. We like it because it offers us the permission to not only do what we want, but say what we like and go where we want – all without anyone's authorization or consent.

The problem I have is that many people do what I call selective growth. They behave grown only when it suits them. I always tell people you can't be grown when you want to have your way and then when something happens you want to be all child-like. Being grown comes with responsibility, independence, accountability and self-regulation.

You don't get to be a child when the bills are due
You don't get to be a child when things are going wrong
You don't get to be a child when you arrive at the crossroads of life
You don't get to be a child when you get yourself into a mess
You don't get to be a child when you offend someone

We live in a world where we do not teach our children consequences. We do not teach our children what it means to have adult responsibilities. So they grow up spoiled, irresponsible and unaccountable. They grow up into adults who do not take responsibility for their actions. They grow up into adults who are child-like about the decisions they make and the impact of those decisions. I will end with the words from that same diva and that same song, "I was spending all my nights and days laid back day dreaming." Time to wake up and be all grown!

Dr. ABC

Word Power # 114: The Good News Doesn't Have To Be About You

When I use to attend church back home in Jamaica, I use to cry a lot. Tears of joy. I cried whenever I saw the "Master's Hands" at work. I cried whenever anyone would testify of God's goodness. Things would be a mess in my life, but when I heard the good news it made me happy. It made me hopeful. It made me confident. I always thought that when I did not get a blessing, it was not that he had forgotten me, but he was just busy blessing someone else!

We have to come to a place in our life when we realize that the good news does not have to be about us for us to be happy and cheerful. We must come to the point when we are authentically happy for others. This is not as easy as it sounds. We will need to work at it. Really work at it. In 2014 when I completed by PhD and sent out invitations to my graduation dinner, I received a text from a former co-worker. She was home for months sick, things were not going as planned and she was being forced out of a job she had for years, her only livelihood:

"Hi Andrew, first and foremost CONGRATULATIONS!!! I am so proud of you that words cannot express my happiness for you! When I opened the envelope and started reading the card I broke down in tears...of joy...It was simply the best news I'd heard in such a long time, and it had to do with someone who is so special to me."

She was going through a very rough time. There was finally good news but it was not for her. She used that opportunity to celebrate someone else.
How do you celebrate others?
Do you even celebrate others?
Do you walk with your pompoms to cheer others?

Remember to be happy for others as much as you are happy for yourself! See what that does to your own happiness! The good news does not have to always be about you.

Dr. ABC

(Dedicated to Kaschka Watson, Stafford Henry, Stephanie Tuters, Keishla Hunt, Otis Burnett and Lorraine Simms who gave me so much help or always had their pom-poms ready, during my doctoral thesis journey, well knowing the good news was not about them.)

Word Power # 115: Come From Under Them

I am happy that I am educated. Not because I want to show off. But because education was my way of getting out from under them. Growing up as a little effeminate boy in a tough neighbourhood was no dolly house. Trust me, I played a lot of dolly house.

I shudder to think of what my life would have been like if I had to wait to be fed by some people
I shudder to think of the pain I would suffer if I had to sleep under the roofs of some people
I quake to imagine what my life would have been like if I had this big personality and lived in someone's box
I am afraid to think of the hurt I would face if I had this big mouth and had to ask for permission to speak

I thank God, each night before I go to sleep, when I think of what my life would have been like if I did not have my own. Today, I see many people being treated like shit by family members and others who have power over them. I hear some sad stories of people who suffer shame and ridicule under the roof of others because they depend on them for their food and shelter. I cry when I hear stories of emotional and verbal abuse being endured by others who must live with family until they get their life together and are able to stand on their own.

Those of you, in that position, must work hard at your ambitions and goals so that you can come from under them. You have no time to waste and procrastinate. You have no time to idle. You have no time to watch every show on TV. You have no time to go to every party and try to be in every fashion.
It is time to be ambitious and determined and come from under them. Set your eyes on your goals. Stay focused. Work hard. Do not live your whole life under the mercies of people who do not have your best interest at heart. Come from under them!

Dr. ABC

Word Power # 116: Glitter On

When someone tells you the things they hear people say about you,
Thank them for the information, Do not waste time to verify,
Reapply your lip gloss
Go on with your day
Let no one allow you to become pissed and bitter and all emotionally caught up. All that stuff makes you age faster, lose your appetite, and give you unnecessary lines and bags under your eyes. Nothing spoils a day like news that you can do absolutely nothing about!
Smile
Glow
Grow
Sprinkle glitter on your day and GO!

Dr. ABC

Word Power # 117: Emotional Rest Stop

I like road trips. I like roads trips because you get to see many sites and scenes, but most of all you can talk as much as you want without worrying about the other passengers.

One of the things I love most on a road trip is getting to a rest stop!
A rest stop is not your destination, it is just a place to use the bathroom and grab a snack

A rest stop is not your place of desire, it is just a place to get gas and stretch your legs

A rest stop is not a place to store things, it is just a place to throw away garbage you have gathered so far on your journey

There are way too many people getting caught up at rest stops not realizing the temporary fix. They fall in love and easily get tricked by those who just come to fill up.

Many people have no intention of making a life time commitment to you. They have a plan and they are on their way to someone else. They meet you and decide to make your heart a rest stop. They are there only for a while. They are there only to refresh and get their groove on.

Don't allow anybody to make your heart their rest stop. You are good enough to wait. I have had times, in the past, when I needed to use the bathroom while travelling and had to hold it until I got where I was going. Don't allow anyone to use you and trick you. Hold it until you get there.

Dr. ABC

Word Power # 118: Feed Me a Lie Please

Why on earth do people want you to FEED them lies so that they can feel good!!! I am always so shocked when people are upset when they ask you a question and you provide them with an honest response...they hate that!!!

Ohhhhhhhhhh Nooooooo

Call the police!!!

Call the ambulance!!!

Call 911 and 119 and all the other emergency numbers!!!

The truth is in trouble - they want you to just tell them a bunch a lies so they can walk away feeling good.

I know honest pills can be hard to swallow, but you are a better person afterwards!

When you ask for feedback, prepare for the truth. It may hurt a bit, sting a little or embarrass for a while – but it will make you healthy.

Dr. ABC

Word Power # 119: Let it Go and Grow, Glow and Go

As a child in primary school, I can remember learning about various types of food. We learned about food that made you go and grow. This was good food. This was the food that provided energy, sustenance and nutrients.
We also learned about the other food that was not good for you – too many sweets, lots of soda and junk food. I really did not like this lesson. I was being told that the things that I liked were not good for me. The things that I desired and wanted to eat, the minute the bell rang, were not good for me.

A week ago, I had a real heart to heart talk with someone who was holding on to something that had obviously eluded him. Something not good for him. It was time to let it go. The only reason why I told him to let it go was because the damage was clear. It was being caused by holding on to something that had already left the station!

What is the use? What are you still hoping for? How long will you stand at the station watching the train speeding away from you? What else can someone say to you to let you know it is goodbye?

We have to learn to let things go and Grow

We have to let it go so we can Glow

We have to let it go so we can Go

Dr. ABC

Word Power # 120: What Do We Say to Our Children?

In the barbershop, a little boy about 7 years old, who seems to be the son of a female employee, is walking like a model up and down the shop.

Barber #1: *"Come here likkle bwoy. Stop walkin' like dat. Yu need a fadda.*

Barber #2: *(Takes the little boy and rubs his head so hard that he begins to cry. He continues to physically "annoy" the little boy.) You need to behave like man!*

The little boy's future of being gay is now the talk among a few of the barbers.
The boy is crying and goes to his mother. His mother comes out of a room, shows her son sharp scissors and advises him to stab the barber on his hand the next time he troubles him.

What are we doing to our children? Who will tell this little boy, who obviously has to grow up among these men, that he has worth? Who will tell him that he is handsome and intelligent? Who will tell him that he is special and his black skin is beautiful? Who will tell him that he has a nice smile and the whitest teeth?

So now, this is what he will get every day, and then finally one day, a man will come along - ANY man - and tell him he is handsome, and he will, for the first time, hear positive words and sleep with that man. Be careful how you speak to our children.

Speak LIFE !!!

Dr. ABC

Word Power # 121: Accomplish Your Resolutions

There are many important messages that I am sure some of you
would have covered with your teachers this month. I, however,
would like to take the next few minutes to talk to you
about **Resolutions**.

Have any of you ever made a resolution?
Do you know what a resolution is?
A resolution is something that you determine you will do and
you have a strong and firm state of mind about it. Simply put -
you know you want to do something and you ensure you get
that thing done. Why do I want to talk to you about resolutions
at this time? You may be saying to yourself, "it is not New Year's
Day" since that is when most of you hear about resolutions. You
may be saying "wow, this man is 2 months late". Yes, I agree, if
we were talking about the traditional New Year's resolutions.
But resolutions are not only about New Year's Day, they
are about deciding what you want to do or want to be or want to
accomplish. Today, as we focus on Black History Month, I want
us to focus on the many resolutions that were made by some
of the greatest black people we know and what they did to
accomplish them.

They fought
They ran away
They worked
They rebelled
They created
They invented
They voted
They sang
They prayed
They stood
They accomplished their resolutions!

Accomplishing resolutions, or goals or your dreams is
not always easy. Many people make resolutions and they end up
breaking them very early. They break them because someone
tells them they are not good enough. They break them because
someone bullied them into doing something else. They break
them because no one else around them has those dreams and
aspirations, so they decide - this dream may be too big for me!
They break them because someone told them –

"You are too black to have that dream"
"Where you come from no one has that dream"
"Who do you think you are having such a big dream?"
"Boys and girls like you don't become doctors,
lawyers, politicians, businessmen, actors, models, designers,
singers"

And some people listen to all of this and then decide - I won't
dream! I won't make a resolution – I won't become somebody!
You must dream. You must make a resolution. You must become
somebody. What is your resolution for your life? What is it that
you desire to become? Think about it.

Dr. ABC
*(Excerpt from Black History Month Speech at Mary Shadd School,
Toronto District School Board, February 24, 2015)*

Word Power # 122: Take Care of Your Blessings

You ask for a job - turn up on time and prepared.
You ask for things - take care of them, clean them and care for them.
You ask for a child - focus on that child, teach and nurture.
You ask for good health - eat right, exercise and do the other deeds.
You ask for good friends - be a good friend first.
You ask for money - stop wasting the little you already have.
You ask to be a teacher - get your lessons ready and be at school before the bell!!
You ask for a vacation - save, plan and prepare for it and then enjoy it - do you!
You ask for rest - get off the phone and get in bed!
Take care of your blessings peeps!!
You are more blessed than you think - just take better care of the blessings you now have and see what happens!!
The truth is, you are a major source in your own blessing.

Dr. ABC

Word Power # 123: Take That Step

There is so much more in you than you know!
This word power is specifically for those who are taking a step
but are a little scared of what may happen.

Take that step.

Better to try and fail than to sit down wondering what may have
been. Yes, I know the unknown is scary and take it from me, I
have been scared many times wondering if I do it.

What will they say if I fail?
What will happen if I come home without it?
What will others say if I did not get it?
What will I do if I do not accomplish it all?

These are the questions that weaken us and disempower us.
These are the questions that stand in our way of trying.
These are the questions we ask ourselves and then retreat
because of fear and doubt.

Take that step today peeps. Nervous and worried and scared and
frightened and shy - take that step!! You did the work. You are
prepared. Take that step.

Dr. ABC

Word Power # 124: Seeking Water

How do you make plans for your dreams and aspirations?
How do you plant seeds?
What do you do after those seeds have been planted?
I am a firm believer in planting seeds – seeds towards your
ambitions, seeds towards your dreams, seeds towards your
passions and goals.
Most people I meet have planted seeds.
The concern I have is with the watering.

Are you watering those seeds or are you just waiting for the
rain?
What if there is a drought?
Are you going to push hard and find other means to water?
Will you dig a well?
Will you hike to the mountain where the spring is at?
How desperate will you be to find water?

Do not just wait for the rain, start digging your own well. Water
your dreams. Water your passion. Water your occupation. Water
your career. Water the next step. Water your promotion. We do
not always feel like watering and we get tired too, but we must
water.

Watered seeds must grow!

Dr. ABC

Word Power # 125: Cry

When was the last time you had a good cry?
The kind of cry that makes you remember your past and measures how far you have come and reminds you how faithful God has been.
The kind of cry that makes you look around you and see what your hands have done and reminds you that there is more for you to achieve, but you should take this one moment to just reflect.
The kind of cry that makes you humble and makes you look into yourself and examine your actions and allows you to purpose in your mind and heart to do better, treat others better, and treat yourself better.
The kind of cry that gushes and rushes as you think of the dark and dangerous places you have been and how much you could have been a "has been" but you are here and present and accounted for.
The kind of cry that reminds you that you are just human and makes you want to be hugged and propped and handled and cushioned – if even for a minute.
The kind of cry that makes you literally feel cleaner on the inside as if the tears literally washed away stains and spots.
It is OK to cry – I dare say, it is healthy to cry.

Dr. ABC

Word Power# 126: Make Them Sad

Growing up, I was called so many names. The kids and their parents who did the name calling knew they were inflicting pain. They knew they would make me cry. They knew they made me scared and afraid. They knew I was afraid of them, when I was in their crowd. The people in church knew that when they whispered about me they would ostracize me. They knew my best friends would not ask me to be in their weddings again. They knew I would not get invited to certain events. They knew that they told their children not to be friends with me. They knew all the names I was called and, as adults, they never intervened.

My mom and I had a real serious talk this summer. She asked me many questions – some I had the answer to and others I needed to really think about. The most impactful part of the discussion was about happiness. Not mine – but the happiness of others based on my personal choices.
I thought long and hard about this part of the discussion and then the simple answer came from me, not in my usual assertive strong manner, but in a low whisper that came from a strong place of inner resolve:
"Mummy, when I was sad and hurt everyone else was happy. Now I am happy and everyone is hurt. Well, I choose my happiness over theirs! Simple!"

There are some people in your life that can only be happy if they know you are sad. They become very sad when they see you being happy. There is also absolutely nothing you can do to make them happy. They have decided what your life should be and what you should do and nothing else that you do will make them happy. I decided that I cannot live my life to make them happy and, at the end of the day, I am sad and incomplete. So, at the end of the day, if I had to choose who will be sad, it would be you and not me. Just the reality.

Dr. ABC

Word Power # 127: Seasons Change

I have a number of pictures of my backyard. They are very different from each other. Some have me alone, some have me with my best friends, others have me hosting an event with lots of people, and others with just family. Those same pictures have the backyard being green and lush, others with the wonderful colourful artwork of leaves that only autumn can bring and others covered in snow and ice - slippery and dangerous.
It is a clear indication of the changing seasons.

Seasons do change in our lives.
What do we do when the seasons of our life change?
What do we do when the fields are not green and lush?
What do we do when the leaves fall off and we are left without?
What do we do when things and dreams and opportunities in our lives get cold and frozen?
How do we prepare for the change?
Are you taken off guard by the change?
Do you just live your life complaining about the change?
Do you embrace the change?
One thing in life is certain and that is change!

Take on the changes head-on. Open yourself to the newness that comes with change.
Things will change in our lives.
We are always excited and ecstatic about those changes that take us to a brighter, higher, better, safer place. It is easy to embrace those changes.
But how do we handle those changes that challenge, chide, expose, uncover, pain and push us?
My strategy is to pray for strength, stamina and staying-power to handle those times in my life when the seasons change.

Dr. ABC

Word Power # 128: Questions Are Good Too

Can we have it all?
Should we have it all?
Is life meant for us to have it all?
I realize how sad and miserable we can be when things are out of our reach.
Do we keep trying for it all?
Do we settle for less?
Should we reach for only those things in our scope or should we look higher, deeper, wider, fuller, stronger and brighter?
Today I have more questions than answers peeps and I come to also understand and appreciate that this is fine.
We cannot have all the answers, but if we are honest and take the time to ask ourselves the questions, then we are actually in a better place, than pretending we do not have unanswered questions.
What are those unanswered, hard, confusing questions that you have?
Ask yourself them - you may be shocked that you actually know the answers.
Why do we ignore the answers?
Would we rather have a different answer?
Do we secretly hope that there is a better answer than the real answer?
Ask yourself those hard questions - before anyone else has to ask you them and then decide if you know the answer before you go about seeking answers.

Dr. ABC

Word Power # 129: Can I have Some More Please?

I recently had a chat with a number of people. They were all in relationships and they concluded that they were
not getting what they wanted from the relationship.
The significant thing was that none of them knew really how to ask for more, demand more or get more. Yes, they spoke to the partner or spouse but after 2 years, 5 years or 10 years, they were still waiting for more!

I was taken aback by this wait.
People will treat you exactly how you have taught them to treat you.
If people know you will always be fine with sardines - they won't offer you salmon.
If the man who beats you knows he can cry and you take him back - he won't stop beating you and won't stop crying so he can get you back.

I wondered what was the issue - why so many people had settled for less than.
I wondered why they believed that they could not get more.
I wondered how they would feel if they discovered that more was possible and available.

Just remember, in a world of bargains and sales - no one will pay more, if you have already discounted yourself!

Dr. ABC

Word Power # 130: I will Jump Out Your Box

Today, I am reminded why I was happy to leave a small island and small spaces where everything is controlled by a small few who still have the plantation mentality, and you must see and respect them as Massa! They keep all the doors closed and only let you in if they like you or you are in their crowd. While living in Jamaica and the Bahamas, I came to this realization and made up in my mind to become a global citizen!!! Small islands are controlled by too many gods who you must kiss their feet to stay in favour.

I am so happy to jump out of their box – let no one put you in their small island/small town box to keep you down. Let no one tell you that your dreams are too big. Let no one devalue your work or worth!

People put people in boxes because they are not in their class.
People put people in boxes because they do not believe in their dreams.
People put people in boxes because they have a lesser expectation of them.

Do not allow people to put you in the box that suits them.
You cannot put me in a box - I will jump out!

Dr. ABC

Word Power # 131: More Than Silver and Gold

We can all pretend with each other and smile always and ignore the real things happening with each other or we can offer to those around us something real.

A hug, a listening ear, a smile, hold their hands for a minute, physically touch them while we talk to them, make a phone call to affirm them, give what we can if and when we can, send a post card to say I am thinking of you, share your dinner etc.

So many people close to us are hurting and, yes, it feels crazy when you cannot help, but I have come to realize that just because we do not always have money or tangible things to offer, we must still know we can help. YES....let no one fool you...a hug, a smile, a chat, a post card, a call, etc. cannot be eaten, cannot pay bills, cannot pay rent etc., but it can help so many people to hold on just a little more, to stand still just a little longer, to believe just some more, to stay away from the ledge, to throw away that rope, close that pill bottle, to get out of bed, to not make that silly mistake.

Yes, I have felt helpless at times when people reach out to me and I cannot help people in real need - but I also know that in those times when I cannot offer silver or gold, they were sent my way because they needed more than silver or gold at that time. Offer to those in need whatever silver or gold you have, but when you have given all, just remember, many people want even more than silver and gold. I pray today that we will have more to offer and when we have given all, we will be reminded that people need other things also - not just silver and gold.

Dr. ABC

Made in the USA
Monee, IL
17 June 2021